No Small Feat
Party Secrets from the Silver Sisters
Stand-Up Entertaining

Children's Home Society of Florida
Gulf Coast Division

Embracing Children. Inspiring Lives.

The Children's Home Society of Florida's vision is to
be a state and national leader in providing high quality community-based solutions
to meet the needs of individuals, families, and communities.

Proceeds from the sale of No Small Feat will be used to provide support
of services and projects of The Children's Home Society of Florida, Gulf Coast Division.

This cookbook is a collection of favorite recipes, which are not necessarily original recipes.

Copyright © 2005
by
Children's Home Society of Florida
Gulf Coast Division
8306 Laurel Fair Circle, Suite 160
Tampa, Florida 33610

Phone: 813.740.4266

www.chsfl.org

ISBN 0-9766623-0-2

WIMMER
COOKBOOKS

A CONSOLIDATED GRAPHICS COMPANY

800.548.2537 wimmerco.com

The Secret Is Love

It all started with a party.

The original event, called The Silver Coffee, was created in 1978 to raise badly needed funds for the Gulf Coast Division of the Children's Home Society of Florida. It began as a stand-up, daytime affair, the hallmark of which was always lavish, time-consuming, personal attention to detail. This party became a community tradition, known for the special quality of its homemade foods and the beauty of the homes in which it was held. After twenty years the committee was ready for a change. The "Moonlight" themed evening party was born using a similar format. It is still stand-up entertaining, but the current event is held at night and includes men!

This cookbook presents many of the recipes that have been served at our parties over the years, and contains creative party menus using these recipes. It also outlines many of the "secret" techniques or bits of knowledge which have made our parties so successful. The real secret, however, is love. Caring friends make it all possible.

The committee of neighbors and friends has grown exceptionally close through the years. We affectionately call ourselves the "Silver Sisters", and spend months planning the party. The week which precedes the party has sometimes been called "organized frenzy". One year two committee members spent twenty-four hours decorating cookies so elaborate that most guests didn't eat them but took them home as souvenirs.

The day before the affair, we gather in our running shoes for the "Cooking Party", where many dishes are perfected and assembled. The warm atmosphere and excitement are exhilarating. We enjoy each other, and enjoy creating good food, inventive libations, and an atmosphere of casual elegance, often prompting observers to say that love is our secret ingredient. We have maintained our unique approach to fundraising – one that would be impossible without the support of loyal friends. We have been fortunate to find so many generous hosts and hostesses who have opened their beautiful homes, not previously used for fundraisers. These lovely homes have provided the ambiance of an intimate personal party. Our guests are very generous in their support of CHS and have helped our committee return over a half-million dollars to the Gulf Coast Division. These donations have made a significant difference in the lives of hundreds of children in need who, with this help, have been provided the gifts of opportunity, hope, and possibility.

The secret really is love…

Sponsored
by
Sandra
and
Craig Barkley

Children's Home Society of Florida

Gulf Coast Division

The Children's Home Society of Florida (CHS) is the state's largest and one of the oldest not-for-profit providers of services to children and families. Founded in 1902 as a Jacksonville orphanage by Rev. D.W. Comstock and the Rev. W.E. Boggs, CHS now operates from more than 204 locations. CHS serves communities all across the state through division offices. The Gulf Coast Division serves 9 counties: Pinellas, Pasco, Hillsborough, Manatee, Polk, Hardee, Highland, DeSoto and Sarasota. The Council on Accreditation of Services nationally accredits CHS for Families and Children, a distinction awarded to less than 1% of child-caring agencies.

The primary goal of CHS services is to strengthen families and keep them together, although not in cases involving a child who might be endangered during the healing process. CHS serves more than 50,000 children and 48,000 adults annually; the Gulf Coast Division serves 3000 children. CHS funding is provided by government contracts (83%), contributions (11%), United Way (5%), and program fees (1%).

Programs administered by the Gulf Coast Division include:

- Adoption and foster care in St. Petersburg

- Recruitment and maintenance of foster homes

- Joshua House in Lutz - residential care facility

- New Beginnings at Joshua House - program for pregnant teens

- Hillsborough Kids Care Management

- Family Visitation House in St. Petersburg

- Child Protection Team located in Bartow

- Children's Advocacy Center

- Hansen Center in Sebring - residential care facility

- School-based services in Manatee

- Special need adoptions in Lakeland

Sponsored by
Kelly and Tom Nash
Liz and Paul Phillips

4

Silver Coffee Committee 2005

Jennifer Andersen
Sandra Barkley
Ernestine Bean
Niki Bouchard
Diane Cagni
Pie Cook
Nicole Doyle
Beth Ann Fisher
Jan Reynolds-Hooks
Irene Hughes
Allison Jester

Shawn Karaphillis
Marie Kudelko
Robin C. Kuebel
Ali Martin
Kelly Nash
Liz Phillips
Melinda Royster
Patricia Slaughter
Sarah Lynn White
Brenda Whitehead

Silver Coffee WOW's and Former Committee Members

Maria Cantonis
Marilyn Connelly
Bette Crown
Delene Crown
Sally Guthrie
Jeanette B. Hale
Chloe Harriman
Nancy Hart
Myra Hemerick
Gay Lancaster
Marilyn Lokey

Susan McKay
Margaret Michaels
Penny Miller
Diane Morse
Jackie Orr
Pat Padgett
Nancy Raymond
Sara Hale Simmons
Martha Thorn
Dorothy Hagan Wice

Acknowledgements

As the title states, entertaining is No Small Feat, but neither is producing a cookbook! Any such project requires the commitment of countless contributors, sponsors, testers, tasters, writers, editors, marketers, and patient families. To all of them, we offer our sincere heartfelt thanks, because no feat is complete without friends and supporters to make the dream a reality.

A special thank you to our Bookmark sponsor.

A special thank you to our friends at Hooters and Pete & Shorty's for underwriting our marketing efforts.

Special Acknowledgements

We are so grateful to Betty Perry and Particus Blackshear, who have been members of our Silver Coffee family since the early days. They have given unselfishly of their time and considerable talents to make every event a success.

Cookbook Development Committee

Sandra Barkley
Gay Lancaster
Marilyn Lokey
Kelly Nash
Liz Phillips

Contents

● ● ● ● ● ● ● ● ● ● ● ● ● ● ● ● ● ● ●

Marilyn ~ Chair
Sandy ~ Development & Marketing
Liz ~ Recipes & Menu Development
Gay ~ Writer & Editor
and
Kelly ~ The Artist

Silver Secrets

The Silver Sisters share tips learned
along the way through more than a
quarter century of entertaining.

Sponsored by
Silver Coffee Committee 2005

Secrets of Gracious Entertaining

- Hospitality is a gift, it comes from the heart.

- Served with flair, even the most simple fare becomes extraordinary.

- When something goes wrong – and something always does – laugh about it and serve another round of drinks.

- Adults of mixed ages add depth and enliven conversation at any gathering.

- Guests notice and appreciate the little extras – cute cocktail napkins, cloth napkins, glassware rather then plastic cups.

- Flowers and/or greens are not an extravagance – they are essential.

- Greet your guests with a smile and something to drink right away.

- Music selection sets the tone – select carefully. Vocals can interfere with dinner table conversation, but are great for cocktails. Start louder; end softer.

Secrets of Special Parties

- Know your guests – young people eat more than older ones. They also drink more, especially beer for younger men.

- Guests eat more at casual parties than at formal affairs.

- When using a caterer, make sure their commercial pans will fit in your oven. You may want to take your own baking dishes for the caterer to use (to assure they will fit in your oven).

- When using a caterer or hosting an event at a private club, don't just turn over all the decisions to them – participate! Discuss your menu ideas, bring some personal recipes, and engage in creative give and take with the chef and/or caterer. By taking these extra steps, a party will evolve which is a reflection of its hosts.

- Attendance at large parties usually has a 10% to 15% attrition factor among those who accept.

- Maintain a "helper list" of people: caterers, kitchen help, servers, bartenders, rental places and musicians.

- Bartenders – plan on one for every 50 to 60 guests.

- Kitchen help – plan on one for every 50 to 60 guests.

- Most liquor stores will accept and refund returned unopened liquor bottles. Discuss this in advance with the vendor.

- Big parties – plan on extra serving pieces - two serving dishes per item, which makes it easier to replenish quickly.

- Prior to the event, label serving dishes and trays with sticky notes so helpers know what food goes where.

9

- Mark the table with sticky notes designating where serving dishes are to be placed.

- Post the menu in the kitchen for helpers to know what is served with what, and at what time.

- Seated dinners require carefully planned seating – clever place cards for small groups, charts or cards for large events. Guests appreciate not having to scramble for seats.

- Mix and match your china. Layer different sets of dishes for a unique look.

- Use ribbon as inexpensive napkin rings and tuck in some greenery for an added touch. Store ribbon in zip-top plastic bags to use year after year. Blow into the bags to puff them; it will protect ribbons and bows.

Secrets of Successful Menus

- Baking is a different skill from cooking – cooking is casual, baking is exact. Understand your personal orientation.

- The better the ingredients, the less you need to do to make the dish taste perfect.

- Kosher salt has large irregular crystals. It is about half as salty as table salt, so use twice as much.

- When a recipe calls for fresh herbs and you only have dried, use half the amount of dried. For instance, if the recipe asks for 2 tablespoons fresh dill, use 1 tablespoon dried dill. Rub it between your palms to release the flavor.

- Use ingredients that are in season when planning your menu. For instance, asparagus in Spring, corn in Summer, and squash in Fall.

- Buy simple, delicious foods for instant hors d'ouevres, and serve them as is. For example: various kinds of olives, bowls of pickled vegetables (asparagus, green beans, cauliflower), large capers with stems, dry roasted edamame beans, specialty cheeses, and fancy nuts. This saves time and makes less to do in advance.

- Freshening bread is easy: Preheat oven to 350 degrees. Place hardened baguettes or other unsliced bread in a paper bag, fold open end to enclose completely, sprinkle with water on all sides, place directly on oven rack and heat 5 to 10 minutes, or until bread is soft and warm. This is also a good method for heating rolls.

- The most popular foods are comfort foods, things everyone loves, served artfully.

- Make one fabulous, over-the-top dish for your dinner party (an appetizer, salad, entrée, or dessert) and fill in with more easily made or purchased items. Guests will still be impressed.

- Assembling food versus cooking or baking? Guests will not enjoy the meal more if you spend days making a difficult dessert, versus purchasing a bakery angel food cake and adding vanilla ice cream topped with fresh fruit or a little Kahlúa and chopped Macadamia nuts.

- Hors d'oeuvres before dinner: plan 5 bites per person (a shrimp, cheese square, meatball, stuffed mushroom, filled pastry, etc.).

Easy Steps To Entertaining

Great parties of any size or style need planning and creativity. These ideas will help you put your best foot forward.

Sponsored by
The Lokey Family
Marilyn, Tom, Michael and Kingsley
In memory of Mary and Mike Meisel —
wonderful parents and grandparents who
taught us the art of entertaining.

Easy Steps to Entertaining

Planning and Organizing

- Create a notebook for all your party information. Include the date of the party, guest list, and types of liquor and wine served. After the party, review your notes and make corrections and future recommendations. It's instructive and fun to look back on parties you have given, and makes preparation easier the next time.

- In your notebook keep an inventory of your silver, fine china, casual china and any other items used for entertaining. This comes in handy when planning a group party or your own large party. When taking your silver to the party site, bag it in zip-top plastic bags with your name and inventory on the bag.

- Shopping – after developing the menu through recipe book and cooking magazine research, gather recipes and make a grocery list. Write down everything you need to buy and determine those items you already have in your pantry.

- Prepare as much as possible in advance. If it can be refrigerated or frozen, make it ahead. Leave as little as possible for the day of the party; you will be much more relaxed.

- A week before the party, check your china and silver, as well as the linens. Make sure the silver is polished and linens are pressed. Decide on serving pieces for each menu item served and place a sticky note on each one.

- Don't forget cocktail napkins. Find those which reflect the party's theme or the colors of your home. We like to keep a supply of paper napkins on hand with a monogram or last name printed on them. For special occasions the ultimate cocktail napkin is, of course, linen.

- Schedule – every party should have a timetable. It helps to work backwards, starting with the time the meal is to be served, and working back to when you expect guests to arrive, including times when items need to be baked or assembled. Post it in the kitchen so you won't forget something.

- Remember you don't have to personally prepare everything you serve. Locate specialty items you can take out. For example, cheese shop, deli, bakery, or even sides or entrées from a restaurant or club.

- If you are organized you can adapt to a crisis more easily.

Entertaining Space

- ## Stand-Up Parties

Use your yard in good weather, but always have a rain plan. Large party congestion usually occurs around the bars, and probably near the entrance at first. Scatter the bars and you'll scatter the crowd. Place one of them the furthest distance from the door. This pulls guests through the space. If there is a super log-jam due to many guests arriving at once, serve glasses of wine on a tray. If the food is pick-up, set up stations in different areas throughout your house. Hors d'oeuvres in the den, main course in the dining room, and desserts on the porch in warm weather.

- ## Seated Parties

If space is limited use the entire house - be innovative! One Silver Sister had guests in her bedroom, and another set up a round table for six in her bathroom. If you need extra tables and chairs, renting is the obvious solution. You can also purchase light-weight table rounds to place over your card table, as well as folding chairs. It's also a good idea to share the costs, usage and storage of party supplies with another couple, or more. A 48-inch round top seats 6 and a 60-inch round top seats 8. If you use rectangular tables, put the most talkative people in the center, which draws the energy of the group to the center of the table. Don't worry about the table being too small. People like to be elbow-to-elbow. Also, people are very willing to eat off their laps, and would often prefer that to being stuck at a table for a prolonged period of time. Consider renting tablecloths and napkins for large parties, or use decorative sheets or discounted fabric to make tablecloths. For napkins, one Silver Sister likes to use terry cloth fingertip towels, which are colorful, washable, and wonderfully absorbent. Use your imagination to find solutions which best suit your needs.

Many hostesses never entertain in their homes because they don't think they have enough space. We think that is nonsense, because creative use of your home, indoors and out will yield space aplenty. Even the smallest home becomes large when outdoor space is incorporated. A rented tent with some twinkle lights can turn an average space into something magical.

Decorations and Ambiance

- Keep apples or lemons in a pretty bowl for an impromptu centerpiece. One step further – poke a few blooms or greens in the bowl among the fruits, encircle it with votive candles, and sprinkle leaves on the table. You have a great look in no time.

- Candles: tea lights or votives (with no scent) for the table. Save the scents for the powder room or entry area.

- Lighting: no bright overhead lighting! Use dimmers or low wattage bulbs.

- White Christmas lights – Don't save them just for the holidays – drape them over a tree or on a fence.

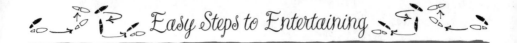

- Candles in jars, hung from ribbons and suspended from tree branches create a lovely, magical glow.

- When designing a centerpiece for a table where guests will be seated, make sure the flowers or decorations don't impede anyone's view. Sit in a chair while you decorate to make sure people can see over the arrangement. Save tall, elaborate centerpieces for the serving tables and entry area.

- Don't clutter the bar with décor. Use a handsome cloth or attractive fabric over a white sheet or rented table skirt on the bar table. And make sure the bartender has plenty of light – good drinks need accurate measurement.

Creative Table Arrangements

- Use three silver or glass cake stands, in graduated sizes. Stack the stands one on top of the other, starting with the largest and ending with the smallest. Place votive candle holders around the perimeter of each stand. If the table is rectangular, arrange various size column candles or extra votives down the middle of the table. Using a paint pen, write each guest's name on a votive cup. Place these votives at each guest's place to serve as place cards. Have all the candles lighted when your guests come to the table. This is very simple to do and presents a wow effect!

- Place a square or rectangular piece of wheat grass from your florist or heath food store in a clear glass or plexiglass tray and let the roots show; or fill a flat container with wheat grass encircled with a wide ribbon. Add water to the container if it is deep enough, or use water soaked oasis under the grass. Punch a few holes in the wheat grass with an ice pick and stick in a few blossoms...voila! A yard in bloom!

- Use square or rectangular short vases and fill the opening entirely with rose, mum, or carnation heads. All one color or complimentary colors are effective. Carnations, which are inexpensive, come in wonderful colors and are perfect for this look.

- Small vases with wonderful little flowers like anemones, cosmos, ranunculus, or sweetheart roses make an interesting look, as do fancy tea cups or sugar bowls, or even pretty jars.

- Place a long sheet of plastic down the middle of your table and cover it with sheet moss and/or mood moss. Arrange little terra cotta pots of herbs throughout the mosses. Place a small miniature rose bush or other small flowering or green plant of a slightly larger scale in the center. Small containers of cut flowers and/or votives may also be placed randomly. For a crisp look, use white flowers in small blue and white containers.

- On a buffet table, a wonderful bowl filled with palm fronds is a simple but sophisticated look. The rhapis palm works well inserted in floral oasis to support the fronds. Napkins can be tied with bear grass for a natural feel, which compliments the look.

- At Christmas time, cover a glass container with cellophane wrapped candy canes, attach them using a glue gun. Tie a red ribbon around the candy canes and place red carnations in the container with just the blooms showing.

- A great way to use extra Christmas tree toppers is to apply hot glue to the bottom of the ornament and glue them to candlesticks. Hot water helps to disassemble.

- A silver bowl of mixed Christmas greens with green grapes nestled in the center can be quite effective. The greens last a long time and flowers can be added (and taken away when they die) throughout the holidays.

- Apples, lemons, limes, or oranges are great holders for tea lights. Use a paring knife to make a circle to accommodate the light. You may need to cut a little off the bottom of the fruit to make it steady.

- Bamboo can be effective in several ways: using plaster of Paris, secure a tall piece of bamboo in the center of a liner pot. Make a fantasy palm using banana leaves, rhapis palm fronds, areca palm fronds, or a mixture thereof. Stick the leaves into the cavity at the top of the bamboo until they hold. Place the liner pot in an urn or cachepot. Arrange oasis around the base of the bamboo for a display of flowers or greenery coming out of the urn. Finally, press a small piece of oasis in the top of the bamboo pole and secure a stem of lady orchids, mimosa, or your choice, for a fun palm tree.

- Cut large blossom flowers short and place them in short containers made of glass, china, or silver. (Examples are lilies, amaryllis, peonies, sunflowers, or dahlias). Julep cups or crystal glasses could also be used. A touch of greens or flowers from your yard may be added. First, place your containers on your table to determine the numbers needed for a rich look. Odd numbers are best.

- Float flowers in one low bowl, or several bowls, with or without floating candles.

How Many Bites?

For appetizers figure:

- Coffee or tea – 4 small savory bites per guest and 2 sweet ones

- Before lunch or dinner – 4 or 5 bites

- Cocktail party – 10 bites

- Reception – 8 cocktail bites and 4 sweet ones

For a two hour party, we figure on 6 to 10 somethings with 2 to 3 being hot and the rest cold, or room temperature. Remember to use a variety of textures from crisp to creamy and a variety of flavors from subtle to spicy.

14

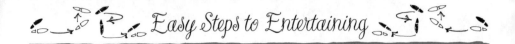

Garnishing – A Few Steps More

- Tie tiny bouquets of herbs or flowers with decorative ribbon or raffia and place them on the corner of serving trays.

- "Found objects", like shells or rocks are great in the center, or in the corner of a tray.

- Small objects, such as Limoges boxes, tiny bud vases, tea cups, or miniature silver items can grace a serving tray.

- Don't forget your yard; many nice fruits, berries and leaves can be found which are appropriate for garnishing. Don't forget to wash them.

- If doilies are used, plan for frequent changes during the course of the party.

- Use cleaned and oiled sea grape leaves, (or other wide, shiny leaves), in lieu of doilies. Think outside the parsley!

- Sliced olives, lemon or lime zest, chopped peppers or squash – all can provide an added festive touch to top off dips or spreads.

- Hollow out fruits and vegetables to contain sauces and dips – or even to hold candles, flowers or greenery.

Buffet Serving

When you have more than 12 guests in your home, it's best to serve buffet style. Guests help themselves, and carry their plates to a table, or sit down with plates on their laps, atop generously sized napkins (20 inch squares, at a minimum). This type of service is conducive to lots of mixing and conversation.

The prime consideration of the buffet should be traffic flow: movement through the serving line should be such that guests who have served themselves need not cross paths with those still in line. In setting up the buffet, think logical progression: plates, followed by the food dishes – light to heavy or first to final courses. Try to use a single serving piece for main dishes, and definitely use tongs for salad to facilitate movement and keep guests from having to put their plates down. We like to have utensils and napkins wrapped together and picked up at the end of the line. We strongly recommend wrapping utensils in napkins which are tied with interesting ribbon or raffia. It looks festive but also keeps your silver from falling out.

When you have an extra-large party, it's a good idea to have duplicate lines on opposite sides of the table to speed food service. Place condiments next to the dish they accompany, but put salt and pepper at the end.

Desserts can be served on the serving table after the main course has been cleared. It's also nice to pass the dessert to save guests from having to get up if the size of the group and logistics permit. Enlist someone to help distribute the plates.

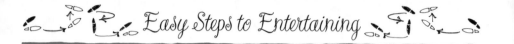

The Bar - Serving Cocktails

- ### Small Casual Parties

Everyone helps themselves. Have set-ups for drinks on a table in an area away from the food service: glasses, beer, wine, liquor, mixers, ice, lemons and limes, as well as a small knife and cutting board, plus spoons for stirring. It's also fun to have one specialty drink, which can be used to reflect the theme of the party, such as a margarita for Tex-Mex food. Remember to provide a non-alcoholic beverage, as well

- ### Larger Parties

Hire an experienced bartender. The rule of thumb is one bartender for every 50 to 60 guests. Once hired, he or she can guide you as to how much beer, wine, liquor and mixers should be purchased. As a guideline, there are 17 – 1½ ounce drinks in a fifth of liquor and about 5 drinks per bottle of wine. Allow three drinks per guest, generally.

It is most important that you assess the guest list and know your crowd. Younger guests in their twenties and thirties are inclined to drink more beer than an older crowd. Guests are trending toward more wine consumption. We've experienced anywhere from thirty per cent to forty-five per cent will drink wine, especially with dinner after traditional cocktails.

If you don't have the space for the proper number of bars or serving areas, have the bartenders make the drinks in the kitchen or the utility room. Then they or other helpers can pass the drink orders among the crowd on small trays. This type of service will require more servers.

- ### Wine

We usually plan on a sixty percent share for white wine and forty percent for red, although red consumption can go to fifty percent when the weather is cool. Generally speaking, Chardonnay is the most popular white wine and Cabernet is the most popular red for party consumption.

When serving wine with a substantial meal, allow about half a bottle per person if you are serving a single wine. If you are serving two wines, count on two glasses of each per person. Fill wine glasses about one-half to two-thirds full, no more, so the bouquet can be appreciated.

- ### Cocktail Napkins

Allow 3 to 4 napkins of high quality paper or cloth per guest.

- ### Glasses

We like to use 9-ounce to 12-ounce stemmed glasses which serve as an all-purpose glass, offering the greatest flexibility. Plan on two glasses per person. If at all possible, don't use plastic glasses indoors. If you must use plastic glasses, count on four per person.

- ### Ice

Don't skimp! Plan on 1½ pounds per person.

Easy Steps to Entertaining

Bar Set-Up For 50 Guests

- ## Liquor

2 liters scotch	750 ml spiced dark rum	750 ml blended whiskey
2 liters vodka	750 ml light rum	750 ml bourbon
1 liter gin		

- ## Mixers

4 liters tonic water	2 six-packs cola	3 liters spring water
3 liters club soda	2 six-packs diet cola	64-ounce cranberry juice
1 liter ginger ale	1 six-pack lemon-lime flavored beverage	64-ounce orange juice
2 liters good sparkling water		64-ounce ruby red grapefruit juice

- ## Garnishes

3 lemons	6 limes	Olives, cherries, cocktail onions

- ## Beer

1 case light beer - long-neck bottles are popular	2-six packs premium beer

- ## Wine

This best estimate is based on a typical crowd (35 to 65 years old) and is for an open bar cocktail party with no dinner served. Consumption will vary with hot and cold weather. One can never be exact, so we always round up. We never return it, but some hosts may want to make that arrangement with the vendor in advance.

Warm Weather:	Cold Weather:
24 bottles Chardonnay	18 bottles Chardonnay
8 bottles Cabernet	14 bottles Cabernet

Lagniappes - Stepping Out

We like to have something for our guests to take home to commemorate a special event or celebration. Instant pictures in special frames – handmade or purchased; Christmas ornament balls with a name painted on them; a small bag of candies, special coffee, or even one large cookie all make great favors to take home. Guests will long remember how special the event was, and the hosts' acknowledgement of their presence.

The lagniappe is especially important for charity events when guests have contributed a significant amount of money to attend. However, the practice of giving lagniappes portrays a generous spirit on the part of the hosts for any special occasion. One example is using small silver frames for place cards. Write each person's name where the picture would go or, even better, put a picture of that person in the frame. When the party is over, the guest takes it home. Another idea is a floral lei for a luau-themed engagement party, or a funny button for round-number birthdays. You do not have to spend a lot – just take some extra steps to show you care.

On-The-Run...?

Let's say you're in a crunch, and, all of a sudden, six people are coming for dinner...eek! If you have an hour, think participation! Grab some meat for the grill, a bottle of interesting marinade, pre-cleaned veggies and salad greens, some fresh fruit, a ready-made unfrosted cake, and lots of wine.

Somebody does the meat marinade, two make the salad, three work the grill (guys love to). One sets the table while you mix up some fruit preserves with liqueur (such as triple sec) to pour over the cake and fresh fruit. Now, everybody is involved, fixing dinner and having fun, because an impromptu dinner has become a party!

Another idea on-the-run is pre-cooked meat, like a roasted or fried chicken, both of which can be carved or plated as they are, or mixed cleverly with salad greens for a main dish.

Keep a list of take-out places. Cruise the grocery aisles for the newest pre-made items. Many stores have cleaned and chopped veggies and fruits; deli sections have side dishes and salads. Bakery sections have nice cakes – just embellish them a little with sauce and ice cream or fruit.

One of the Silver Sisters remembers thoroughly enjoying dinner with one hostess who served beans and franks, along with drinks and a salad. It was done with flair and warm hospitality which, in the end, is all that matters when you entertain.

Remember, we all love to be invited to share time with friends. Don't let limited preparation time or a small pocketbook keep you from entertaining.

Potluck Entertaining

People want to be together, are happy to help, and love a party in someone else's home. Entertaining potluck-style is one of the easiest ways to welcome friends and family to your table. A potluck's beauty lies in the simple division of labor and the joy of sampling someone else's treasured recipes. It's easiest if the host provides the main course – steak or chicken on the grill, for example, or a meat casserole. Assign different side dishes to your guests – hors d'oeuvre, salad, vegetable, starch or dessert. Asking friends to help brings everyone together as a team, and bringing one marvelous dish is easy when you have only that one to make. It's a community, it's collaborative, and it's so much fun, not to mention less intimidating for the hosts and hostesses.

A Host of Hostesses

Several hostesses frequently join efforts for larger parties like pre-wedding parties or showers, baby showers, or children's parties. Together the hostesses decide in whose home the party is to be held, or whether it is to be outside the home. Duties for the party should be shared or allocated so each hostess has equal responsibility in the planning and production of the party. If someone is a great cook have them put the menu together. If another is good at arranging flowers, put them in charge of decorations. Use the group members' individual talents, and you'll end up with a fabulous party. (Usually the hostess whose home is being used is left off the duty list; it is enough for her to get her home ready.)

If you decide to do all the cooking rather than a catered menu, try to even out the food preparations. Non-cooks can assemble the bar, arrange for outside help or, in some cases, purchase food prepared by others and absorb some or all of the cost themselves, for the privilege of not having to cook. A word to the wise: if something is not your job, don't interfere unless you're asked!

It is important that all the hostesses' names appear on the invitation. Guests are greeted by all the hostesses as they arrive, or if there are multiple couples, at least the home hosts, while others help move guests through the rooms, taking purses or coats and pointing out bars and bathrooms. It is imperative that all hostesses stay until the end of the event, and all clean-up is completed or scheduled for the next day. We have discovered over time that tired committee members make poor cleanup partners. Sometimes it's best to begin anew the next morning in order to not prolong the home hosts' misery.

Finances are important. Each host/hostess keeps track of their expenses, with receipts if possible. One host collects receipts and sends out statements indicating who owes whom. Paying all the help should not be just one host's responsibility; decide who will write checks prior to the party, being mindful to distribute expenses as evenly as possible.

Clean-Up

Drop dirty silverware in a bowl of hot, soapy water. After the party you can either wash and dry it, or drain and re-cover it with plain hot water to wait until morning. Don't let washed silver drain dry or it will spot.

Wash and dry wine glasses or crystal by hand. When washing fine china with gold or silver trim and sterling silver flatware, we have found washing in the dishwasher without detergent does an excellent job. The scalding water cleans them beautifully.

Soak napkins overnight in a basin of hot water with pre-wash solution added. The next day you can dump them in the washing machine. Treat red wine stains before you go to bed. Rub them with wet salt and leave them until morning (they need at least 6 hours). Club soda is also good for removing red wine stains.

Sips

Delectable drinks and lively
libations will highlight any occasion.

Sponsored by

LANCASTER
INSURANCE, INC.

Sips

Beautiful Bride

Lemon wedge
Pink sanding sugar

2 ounces vodka
½ cup pulp-free pink lemonade

Rub lemon around rims of two martini glasses and dip in sugar. Fill a cocktail shaker with ice, add vodka and lemonade. Shake well and strain into glasses.

SERVES 2

Bloody-Good Maria

18 ounces tomato juice
12 ounces vodka
6 tablespoons bread and butter pickle juice
6 tablespoons pepperoncini (Greek pepper) juice

1 tablespoon Dijon mustard
1 tablespoon prepared horseradish
1 teaspoon Worcestershire sauce
1 teaspoon hot sauce
1 lime, squeezed

In a large container mix together tomato juice, vodka, pickle juice, pepperoncini juice, mustard, horseradish, Worcestershire, hot sauce, and lime juice. Refrigerate for at least 4 hours. Serve "up" in chilled glasses or over ice, as desired.

SERVES 12

• •

Secret: Freeze lemon peel in ice cube trays with a water-lemonade mixture.

• •

Blush Bellini

A few raspberries give these drinks their vibrant color. Blending the peach purée the day before makes last-minute drink prep a snap. Simply add Champagne as people show up.

1½ cups thawed frozen sliced peaches
1 cup peach nectar
½ cup sugar

¾ cup frozen orange-peach-mango concentrate, thawed
3 frozen or fresh raspberries
3 750-ml bottles chilled Champagne

Combine peaches, peach nectar, sugar, fruit concentrate, and 3 raspberries in a food processor fitted with the metal blade. Blend mixture until smooth. Strain fruit purée into a bowl, stirring to extract as much liquid as possible. Cover and refrigerate until ready to use. (Can be made one day ahead.) When ready to serve, pour ⅓ cup fruit purée into each Champagne flute. Fill flutes with Champagne, stir gently.

SERVES 12

Clearwater Harborita

1 (6-ounce) can frozen limeade	¼-½ cup triple sec
1 cup good tequila	Ice

Pour limeade, tequila, and triple sec into a blender. Fill blender to the top with ice. Blend until thick and icy. Serve immediately or freeze.

ONE BLENDER SERVES 6 TO 8 SMALL CUPS OR 4 TO 6 TEQUILA GLASSES.

> **T**o prepare ahead for a large party,
> make up several batches and store in gallon-size water jugs
> in the freezer. When ready to serve, allow to defrost
> slightly or just until easily poured.

Cranberry Daiquiri

½ cup sugar	½ cup light rum
½ cup water	6 tablespoons dark rum
1 cinnamon stick	6 tablespoons light rum
½ teaspoon grated orange peel	Cranberry juice
½ cup cranberries	Lemon juice

Put sugar and water in a medium saucepan and cook over medium heat until sugar dissolves. Add cinnamon stick and orange peel and bring to a boil. Mix in cranberries and cook until cranberries begin to pop. Remove from heat and cool. Remove cinnamon stick and pour mixture into a jar. Add ½ cup light rum and refrigerate.

When chilled, strain syrup into a pitcher, reserving cranberries. Add dark rum, light rum, cranberry juice and lemon juice to the pitcher. Refrigerate until well chilled.

Serve in Martini glasses that have been filled with crushed ice. Garnish with reserved cranberries.

SERVES 6

• •
Secret: For the Cool Weather Warm Hearth Supper double recipe.
• •

Cranberry, Tangerine, and Pomegranate Champagne Punch

1   package (12-ounces) fresh cranberries (for swizzle sticks)
1   bunch fresh mint (for swizzle sticks)
2   cups pomegranate juice
3   cups tangerine juice

5   cups cranberry-juice cocktail
2   bottles (750 ml each) chilled Champagne or other sparkling wine (such as Prosecco)

To make swizzle sticks, spear 3 cranberries alternately with 2 mint leaves on wooden skewers. Place skewers on a baking sheet and cover with damp paper towels. Refrigerate up to an hour.

In a large punch bowl or pitcher, stir together fruit juices. Fill glasses with ice, and ladle or pour about ½ cup punch into each glass. Top with Champagne. Garnish each glass with a swizzle stick.

SERVES ABOUT 20

• •

Secret: You can purchase pomegranate and tangerine juice at the grocery store.

• •

Cream Sickle

A delicious drink perfect for sipping by the pool or ocean.

1½ ounces amaretto
1½ ounces orange juice

1½ ounces milk

Pour amaretto, orange juice, and milk into a cocktail shaker with ice. Shake and strain into an old-fashioned glass filled with ice.

SERVES 1

Frosted Bellini

1   (750-millilter) bottle Champagne
2   (11.5-ounce) cans peach nectar

½   cup peach schnapps

Combine Champagne, peach nectar, and schnapps in a large pitcher. Stir until well blended. Serve immediately in glasses over crushed ice or pour mixture into a 9 x 13-inch pan, cover, and freeze until firm. Defrost slightly when ready to serve, and pour into glasses.

MAKES 6 CUPS

Frozen Strawberry Daiquiri

1 (12-ounce) can frozen limeade
1 (12-ounce) can light rum or vodka
1 (10-ounce) package frozen strawberries

Ice
Fresh strawberries, for garnish

Pour limeade, rum or vodka, and strawberries into a blender, mix well. Add ice to within 1-inch of the top of the blender. Blend slowly until ice is pulverized and the mixture is thick and icy. Serve in cocktail glasses and garnish with a fresh strawberry.

SERVES 8

• •

Secret: Change the flavor by changing the fruit. Try raspberries or peaches, or leave the fruit out for a traditional lime daiquiri.

• •

Hummer

Forget dessert – save room for this sophisticated after-dinner drink.

1 ounce Kahlúa
½ ounce white rum
½ ounce brown crème de cacao

2-3 scoops vanilla ice cream
Whipped cream
Ground nutmeg

Combine Kahlúa, rum, and crème de cacao in a blender. Add scoops of vanilla ice cream and blend just until mixed. Do not over-blend as the mixture will liquefy. If it becomes too watery, add ice cream and blend until the correct consistency is achieved (it should be thick like a milk shake). Serve in a large stemmed cocktail glass. If desired, top with whipped cream and sprinkle with nutmeg.

SERVES 1

Iced Teaquila

This fruity drink packs a pleasing wallop! Just ask one Silver Sister's daughter.

½ cup sugar
½ cup water
3 tablespoons fresh lemon juice
1 cup guava nectar

2 cups brewed tea
¾ cup silver tequila
Lemon twists for garnish

In a small saucepan, combine sugar and water. Stir mixture as it comes to a boil over medium-high heat. Continue to stir until sugar is dissolved. Let cool to room temperature. Stir in lemon juice. In a pitcher combine lemon syrup, guava nectar, tea, and tequila. Serve in tall glasses over ice. Garnish with a lemon twist.

SERVES 6

Kir

⅔ ounce crème de cassis   White wine, chilled

Pour crème de cassis in a wine glass and fill with white wine.

SERVES 1

● ●

Secret: Make a Kir Royale by using Champagne instead of white wine.

● ●

Make-Ahead Manhattans

⅔ cup blended whiskey   1 glug Grand Marnier
⅓ cup sweet vermouth   Maraschino cherries, for garnish
4 good shakes bitters

Pour whiskey, vermouth, bitters, and Grand Marnier in a cocktail shaker or small pitcher and blend well. Serve in cocktail glasses and garnish with a cherry.

SERVES 4

● ●

Secret: If you triple this recipe, it can be
stored in a 750 ml bottle in your freezer for future use.

● ●

Merry Mistress

2 ounces citron vodka   1 ounce grapefruit juice
1 ounce blue Curaçao   Splash club soda
1 ounce pineapple juice

Fill a cocktail shaker with ice and combine vodka, blue Curaçao, pineapple juice, and grapefruit juice. Shake well and strain into a cocktail glass. Top with a splash of soda.

SERVES 1

Mint Julep

¼ cup bourbon
1 tablespoon mint syrup

Fresh mint sprigs, for garnish

Combine bourbon and mint syrup. Serve immediately in a julep cup over crushed ice. Garnish with mint sprigs.

SERVES 1

Mint Syrup
This makes enough for 44 juleps. Store any leftover syrup in the refrigerator, and use to sweeten iced tea or make other drinks.

1½ cups coarsely chopped fresh mint
2 cups sugar

2 cups water

Tie mint in a cheesecloth bag or metal tea strainer. Place in a saucepan; add sugar and water; bring to a boil. Cook, stirring constantly, until sugar dissolves. Remove from heat, cover, and let cool. Remove and discard cheesecloth bag.

MAKES 2¾ CUPS

Peach-Riesling Sangría

1 (1 pound) bag frozen peach sections
5 ounces peach brandy

1 (750-ml) bottle chilled Riesling
1 (5.5-ounce) can peach nectar

In a large pitcher combine peaches, brandy, Riesling, and peach nectar. Mix together until well blended. Serve chilled.

MAKES ABOUT 2 QUARTS

Red Rooster

1 quart cranberry juice
1 large (10-ounce) can frozen orange juice

3 orange juice cans of water
2 quarts vodka

Mix cranberry juice, frozen orange juice, water, and vodka together and freeze in a gallon-size water jug. Remove from freezer a short while before serving, allowing it to defrost.

SERVES 24

Pearl Diver Martini

The year we did our Pacific Rim Party, these were a huge hit! We were serving
over 200 guests, so we put the martinis in a drink canister with a spigot. People loved it!

1½ cups cracked ice or 6 ice cubes
2   ounces ginger vodka

½   ounce premium sake, chilled
1   slice candied ginger for garnish

Fill a cocktail shaker with ice and add vodka. Shake vigorously to chill. Strain vodka into a chilled glass. Slowly pour in sake, floating it on top of the vodka. Garnish with a candied ginger slice, balanced on the rim of the glass.

SERVES 1

• •

Secret: For the Pacific Rim Dinner make 16 drinks using
1 quart (4 cups) ginger vodka and 1 cup sake.

• •

To make ginger vodka, place 1 cup thinly sliced fresh ginger
into a glass container, add 1 liter vodka, and cap tightly. Let stand at room
temperature for up to 4 days, shaking the container gently every so often.
Using a funnel and a fine-mesh strainer, strain the mixture back into the
original vodka bottle. Cap tightly, label, and refrigerate until ready to serve.

Rosé Apéritif

This is so pretty it should be served in a glass pitcher.

2   cups blueberries
2   cups blackberries
2   cups strawberries, hulled
2   cups raspberries

1   tablespoon sugar
5   ounces Framboise (raspberry liqueur)
1   bottle chilled rosé wine
1⅓ cups white cranberry juice

In a pitcher, combine the blueberries, blackberries, strawberries and raspberries. Stir in the sugar and add the Framboise. Let stand at least 1 hour. Stir in the chilled rosé wine and cranberry juice. Sweeten with more sugar, if desired. Serve chilled.

MAKES 2 QUARTS

Pink Peach Champagne Punch

Ice Ring
- Distilled water
- Decorative fruits (strawberries or cranberries, lemon, lime, and orange slices)
- Fresh mint leaves
- White cranberry juice or white grape juice

Punch
- 1 bottle fruity white wine (like Chardonnay)
- 1 bottle brandy
- 2 quarts cranberry juice
- 2 cups peach schnapps
- 1 bottle Champagne
- 1 quart lemon-lime soft drink

Ice Ring

Two days before the party, pour 1-inch of distilled water in a ring mold and freeze. One day before the party, layer decorative fruits and mint leaves upside down on the ice, and pour 3 to 4 inches of either white cranberry juice or white grape juice over fruit and freeze. When ready to serve, unmold the ice ring and place it decorative side up in a punch bowl. Pour punch into the bowl over the ice ring.

Punch

Chill all punch ingredients overnight before mixing. Combine wine, brandy, cranberry juice, and peach schnapps in a large container. When ready to serve, add the Champagne and soft drink. Pour punch into the bowl over the ice ring.

MAKES 30 TO 34 PUNCH CUPS

● ●

Secret: For the Southern Silver Coffee double recipe.

● ●

Smiling Groom

- ½ cup grapefruit juice
- ½ cup guava juice
- 1½ ounces fresh lemon juice
- 1 tablespoon superfine sugar or powdered sugar
- ½ cup club soda
- 4 ounces gold tequila
- 2 ounces lemon liqueur
- Lemon slice or twist for garnish

Combine grapefruit juice, guava juice, lemon juice, sugar, club soda, tequila and lemon liqueur in a blender. For a frozen drink, blend ingredients adding 10 to 12 ice cubes. For a non-frozen drink, blend ingredients together and pour over ice in a tall glass. Garnish with a lemon slice or twist.

MAKES 4 MARTINI GLASS PORTIONS OR 2 TALL GLASSES

Special Iced Tea

Tea is full of antioxidants and has half the caffeine of coffee.
This is a refreshing combination, easy to make, and good for you.

½ gallon water
1 family-size tea bag
3 orange and sweet spice flavored tea
  bags (Constant Comment)

Lemon wedges, for garnish
Mint sprigs, for garnish

Fill a ½-gallon container with water. Place the tea bags in water and let brew at room temperature for several hours. When tea has finished brewing, remove tea bags and refrigerate. Serve over ice with a wedge of lemon and a mint sprig.

SERVES 8

> **W**e made this refreshing concoction for many
> of our daytime parties. When making it for a large crowd,
> use gallon-size water jugs, and carefully push tea bags into
> top of jug. Brew overnight then refrigerate.

Stoli-Doli

Watch out, this drink packs a punch!

Fresh pineapples
Vodka

Large Mason jar with a tap at the
  bottom (these jars are sold for serving
  iced tea)

Find very fresh pineapples, remove the peel and cut into ½-inch slices. Stack pineapple slices into the large Mason jar. Fill the jar to the edges and rim with pineapple slices. Fill the jar with vodka (Stoli or your favorite brand). Let stand 5 or 6 days. Refrigerate the jar for 6 to 12 hours before serving and pour directly from the tap into martini glasses. If you can't chill the Mason jar, pour the martini from the tap into a shaker with ice, shake and serve as you would a regular martini. Use some pineapple for garnish, if desired.

DEPENDS ON THE SIZE OF THE MASON JAR

Two Cup Cosmos

This is a great drink to have on hand in your freezer.

1 cup citron vodka
½ cup Cointreau

¼ cup Rose's lime juice
½ cup cranberry juice

Measure the vodka, Cointreau, and lime juice into a 2-cup glass measuring cup. Fill to the top with cranberry juice (approximately ½ cup). Store in the freezer until ready to drink. Pour into martini glasses and garnish with a twist of lime.

SERVES 4 TO 5

Muy Mojitos

As refreshing as a summer breeze!

12 ounces light rum
4 ounces mint syrup (see Mint Julep recipe)
4 ounces fresh lime juice
2 ounces sparkling mineral water

6 fresh mint sprigs
6 (2-inch) lemon peels (no white pith)
Crushed ice

Mix rum, mint syrup, lime juice and sparkling water in a pitcher. Pour into glasses of crushed ice and garnish with mint sprigs and lemon peel that has been twisted over the glass to release the flavor.

SERVES 6

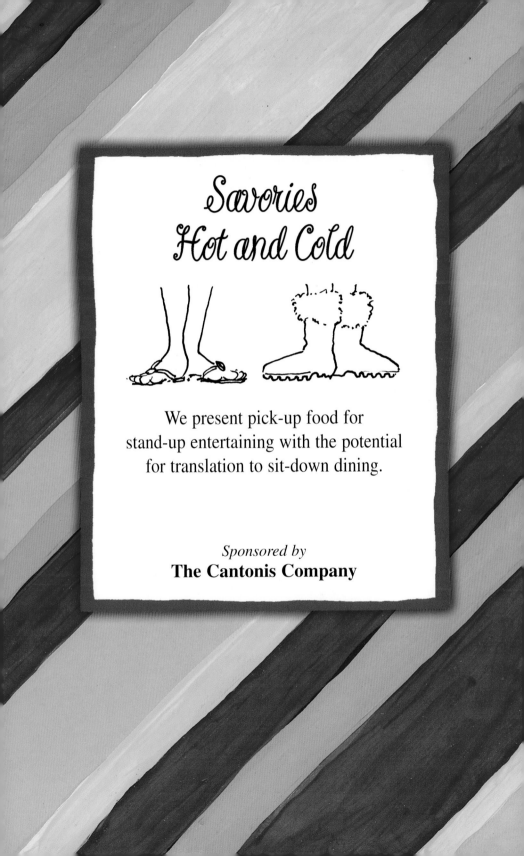

Savories
Hot and Cold

We present pick-up food for
stand-up entertaining with the potential
for translation to sit-down dining.

Sponsored by
The Cantonis Company

Savories~Hot & Cold

Good-For-You Rosemary Nuts

These nuts are "to die for" with their sweet rosemary fragrance.

2   cups (8-ounces) pecan halves, unsalted
2   cups (8-ounces) shelled walnuts, unsalted
1   can (6-ounces) whole natural almonds, unsalted

2¼ tablespoons butter, melted
2   tablespoons crushed dried rosemary
1   teaspoon cayenne pepper
4   teaspoons dark brown sugar
4   teaspoons kosher salt

Preheat oven to 350 degrees.

Place pecans, walnuts, and almonds in a large bowl. Pour melted butter over nuts, mixing well to coat. In a small bowl, combine rosemary, cayenne, brown sugar, and salt. Sprinkle rosemary mixture over nuts and mix together well. Spread nuts in a single layer on a cookie sheet. Toast in the oven about 10 to 12 minutes or until they become golden brown. Be careful not to burn. Serve warm or at room temperature.

MAKES 5 CUPS

Hot-Sweet Almonds

3   tablespoons peanut oil
2   cups whole blanched almonds
½   cup sugar
1½ teaspoons salt

1½ teaspoons ground cumin
1   teaspoon hot pepper flakes, crushed
1   tablespoon sugar

Heat oil in a heavy skillet over medium-high heat. Add almonds and sprinkle ½ cup sugar over them. Sauté until almonds become golden brown and sugar caramelizes. Remove almonds from skillet and place in a bowl. Add salt, cumin, pepper flakes, and 1 tablespoon sugar and mix well. Serve warm or at room temperature. Store in an airtight container.

MAKES 2 CUPS

● ●

Secret: For the Southern Silver Coffee double the recipe.

● ●

Marinated Olives

1 (8-ounce) jar large, brine cured green olives
1 (8-ounce) jar large, brine cured black olives
5 large garlic cloves, crushed
3 large shallots, sliced thin
½ cup Sambuca

¼ cup extra virgin olive oil
1 teaspoon grated orange zest
1 teaspoon minced fresh thyme leaves
1 teaspoon red pepper flakes
¾ teaspoon salt
Pinch cayenne pepper

Drain the olives and rinse well with water. Drain olives of excess water. Combine garlic, shallots, Sambuca, olive oil, orange zest, thyme, red pepper flakes, salt, and cayenne pepper in a glass or other nonporous bowl. Stir in drained olives. Place in an airtight container and refrigerate for at least 12 hours. May be kept in the refrigerator for at least a month.

MAKES 2 CUPS

Barbecued Shrimp

8-10 pounds jumbo shrimp, shells on
1 pound (4 sticks) butter
1 pound (4 sticks) margarine
6 ounces Worcestershire sauce
8 tablespoons finely ground black pepper

1 teaspoon ground rosemary
4 lemons, sliced
1 teaspoon Tabasco sauce
4 teaspoons salt
2-4 cloves garlic, chopped

Preheat oven to 400 degrees.

In a saucepan melt butter and margarine. Add Worcestershire, pepper, rosemary, lemon slices, Tabasco, salt, and garlic and mix thoroughly. Divide shrimp between two large shallow pans and pour sauce over each pan of shrimp and stir well. Bake about 15 to 20 minutes, turning once. Shells should be pink and the meat white (not translucent).

SERVES 16 TO 20

Ceviche

1 pound white fish, chopped into bite-size pieces
7 limes, juiced
1 small white onion, chopped
1 (6-ounce) jar sliced pimento green olives, drained

2 (10-ounce) cans Ro-tel tomatoes, drained
2 tablespoons red wine vinegar
1 tablespoon olive oil
Pinch dried oregano
Pinch cumin
Tortilla chips

Place chopped fish in a bowl. Squeeze lime juice over fish and mix well. Add onion, olives, tomatoes, vinegar, oil, oregano, and cumin. Mix together well. Place in an airtight container and refrigerate overnight. (It is important to refrigerate overnight because the lime juice "cooks" the fish.) Serve with tortilla chips.

SERVES 12 TO 16 AS AN APPETIZER

Conch Fritters with Bahamian Sauce

¾-1	pound (approximately 1½-2 cups) conch, cubed
1	medium onion, minced
2	eggs, slightly beaten
½	cup flour
½	teaspoon salt
1	teaspoon baking powder
¼	teaspoon hot sauce
1	teaspoon good fish seasoning
½	teaspoon Worcestershire sauce
1	teaspoon lemon juice
1	cup seasoned Italian bread crumbs
	Seasoned Italian bread crumbs
	Good vegetable or peanut oil

Wash conch thoroughly in water to which a little vinegar has been added. Rinse the clean, white meat in salted water and drain. Cut off the hard end pieces, keeping only the soft part of the conch. Cut remaining soft meat into pieces and place in a food processor fitted with the steel blade. Add onion, eggs, flour, salt, baking powder, hot sauce, fish seasoning, Worcestershire sauce, lemon juice, and bread crumbs to the food processor. Using the pulse button, turn on and off, mixing thoroughly. Don't over process. Conch should remain chunky.

Form mixture into balls about the size of a quarter. Roll conch mixture in additional seasoned crumbs. Heat oil in deep fat fryer to 375 degrees. Lower fritters into the hot oil, a few pieces at a time. Fry until golden brown on all sides. Remove and drain on paper towels. Serve hot with Bahamian sauce.

SERVES 20 TO 25 FOR APPETIZERS

Bahamian Sauce

½	cup mayonnaise
2	tablespoons Dijon mustard
2	tablespoons ketchup
2	tablespoons Pickapeppa sauce
1	teaspoon lime juice

Combine mayonnaise, mustard, ketchup, Pickapeppa sauce, and lime juice in a mixing bowl and whisk together until thoroughly blended. Store in an airtight container and refrigerate until needed.

MAKES ¾ CUP

Coquille St. Jacques in Phyllo Cups

This unique presentation makes Coquille St. Jacques into a bite-size pick-up hors d'oeuvre.

Scallops

1½	pounds bay scallops	¼	teaspoon salt
½-¾	cup vermouth	⅛	teaspoon white pepper
1	tablespoon chopped shallots or green onions		Pimento stuffed olive slices, for garnish

Sauce

	Reserved cooked liquid	4	tablespoons olive juice
1	cup heavy cream	1	tablespoon all-purpose flour
1	tablespoon olive oil	4	tablespoons (½ stick) butter, softened

Phyllo Cups

8	sheets frozen phyllo pastry or purchased frozen phyllo cups, thawed	½	cup (1 stick) butter, melted

Scallops

Wash the scallops. Bring vermouth, shallots, salt, and pepper to a boil in a large saucepan. Add scallops, reduce heat immediately and simmer for 30 seconds. Remove scallops with a slotted spoon, place in a bowl, and reserve cooked liquid. Cover and refrigerate scallops.

Sauce

Cook reserved liquid in saucepan over high heat until reduced by half. Add cream and boil rapidly until cream is reduced and the consistency of syrup. Add olive oil and olive juice. Combine flour and 4 tablespoons softened butter to make a paste. Add to sauce. Reduce heat and stir until very smooth. May be made a day ahead. Place plastic wrap directly on the sauce, cover and refrigerate until ready to use.

Phyllo Cups

Preheat oven to 350 degrees.

Place one sheet of phyllo onto a smooth, dry surface (keep remaining phyllo covered with plastic wrap and a damp towel at all times). Lightly brush phyllo with melted butter. Layer 3 more sheets of phyllo on first sheet, brushing each one with butter. Repeat to make another stack of 4 sheets of phyllo. Remember to keep prepared stacks covered with plastic wrap and damp towel at all times.

Brush miniature muffin cups with melted butter. Uncover one phyllo stack at a time and cut each stack into 3-inch squares. Place one square of layered phyllo into each muffin cup, pressing gently in center to form a pastry shell. Bake for 8-10 minutes or until golden. Gently remove from pan and let cool on wire racks. Phyllo shells may be made up to 2 days in advance. Store in an airtight container at room temperature.

Coquille St. Jacques in Phyllo Cups continued

Assembly

Place three scallops into each phyllo cup and fill cup ¾ full with sauce. Garnish with an olive slice. Microwave for 30 seconds.

MAKES APPROXIMATELY 24

Crayfish Étouffée

*A true Creole tradition, full of flavor. Ordering the
crayfish fat from a specialty supplier is a worthwhile extra step.*

½ cup butter	**Salt and pepper**
1 cup chopped green onion	**Creole seasoning, to taste**
¼ cup chopped parsley	2 **cups long-grain rice, cooked**
2 pounds crayfish tails	**(enough to serve 8 to 10)**
1 pound crayfish fat or 1 cup butter	**Lemon slices**

Melt butter in a large skillet. Add green onion and cook until tender, about 10 to 14 minutes. Add parsley, crayfish tails, crayfish fat or butter, salt, pepper, and Creole seasoning, to taste. Cook over medium heat 15 to 20 minutes. Serve over cooked rice and garnish with lemon slices.

SERVES 8 TO 10

• •

Secret: For the New Orleans Brunch make recipe 3 times.

• •

Crab Cakes with
Caper Mayonnaise or Mango Salsa

1 pound lump crabmeat (about 2½ cups), order the best
2 cups fine fresh bread crumbs, divided
2 eggs, well beaten
1 tablespoon Dijon or Creole mustard
½ teaspoon Worcestershire sauce
2 tablespoons finely chopped parsley
¼ cup finely chopped green onion
1 teaspoon seafood seasoning (Old Bay)
2 tablespoons capers
½ cup mayonnaise
   Corn, peanut or vegetable oil for fryer
   Caper Mayonnaise or Mango Salsa
   (recipes follow)

In a large bowl mix together crabmeat, 1½ cups bread crumbs, eggs, mustard, Worcestershire sauce, parsley, green onions, seafood seasoning, capers, and mayonnaise. Blend gently together leaving the crab lumps as large as possible.

Using 2 or 3 tablespoons of the mixture, shape into portions of equal size and flatten each into a patty. Coat each patty with remaining bread crumbs. Refrigerate until ready to cook.

To cook, put oil in fryer and heat to 365 degrees. When ready, place 3 to 4 patties into deep fat and cook 1 to 2 minutes or until golden brown on both sides. Drain on paper towels. Serve hot with a dollop of Caper Mayonnaise or Mango Salsa.

MAKES 35 PATTIES

Caper Mayonnaise

2 cups mayonnaise
½ cup sour cream
3 tablespoons capers, well drained
1½ teaspoons fresh lemon juice

In a medium bowl mix together mayonnaise, sour cream, capers, and lemon juice. Place in an airtight container and refrigerate until ready to use.

MAKES 2½ CUPS

• •

Secret: For the Special Occasion Reception double recipe.

• •

Mango Salsa

2 cups diced ripe mango
1 cucumber, peeled, seeded and chopped
½ poblano chili, seeded and finely chopped
1 jalapeño chili, seeded and minced
2 teaspoons minced fresh ginger

¼ cup chopped fresh mint or cilantro leaves
1 tablespoon packed light brown sugar
¼ cup fresh lime juice
   Salt and freshly ground black pepper,
   to taste

Combine mango, cucumber, poblano chili, jalapeño chili, ginger, cilantro or mint, brown sugar, lime juice, salt, and pepper in a mixing bowl and gently toss to mix. Correct the seasonings, adding salt, lime juice, and sugar to taste. The salsa should be a little sweet and a little sour. Mango salsa tastes best served a couple of hours after making. Place in an airtight container and refrigerate until serving time.

MAKES 2 TO 2½ CUPS

Pickled Shrimp

8 pounds large shrimp, cooked, peeled and deveined (may use frozen; thaw according to
   package directions)

Marinade

3 cups white vinegar
3 cups vegetable oil
1 cup olive oil
1 jar (1.5-ounces) pickling spices
1 tablespoon kosher salt
2 tablespoons hot sauce
2 tablespoons celery seeds

2½ tablespoons grated lemon rind
   (use a rasp grater)
6 cups very thinly sliced onions
20 bay leaves
8 tablespoons capers
9 lemons, thinly sliced

Marinade

In a large bowl, whisk together vinegar, vegetable oil, olive oil, pickling spices, salt, hot sauce, celery seeds and lemon rind.

Assembly

Place cooked or thawed shrimp in a large container. Pour marinade over shrimp and mix well. Add sliced onions, bay leaves, capers, and lemon slices to shrimp. Gently mix to combine. Cover well and refrigerate overnight. Serve pickled shrimp slightly chilled.

SERVES 60 AS AN HORS D'OEUVRE

• •

Secret: Most seafood markets will not charge for cooking shrimp, but will charge a per pound fee to peel and devein. If you are in a hurry or to make things easier, this is well worth the cost.

• •

Fried Grouper with Tropical Tartar Sauce

Marinade
1   (8-ounce) bottle French dressing   1   onion, chopped

Fish
2   pounds grouper or snook, cut into strips
    2-inches wide

Batter
1   cup biscuit baking mix   ¼   teaspoon salt
1   egg, beaten   Beer, opened and at room temperature
½   teaspoon baking powder   1   (64-ounce) bottle good vegetable oil

Marinade
Combine French dressing and chopped onion for the marinade. Soak prepared fish in the marinade at room temperature at least an hour before frying.

Batter
Combine biscuit mix, egg, baking powder, and salt, adding beer as needed to make the consistency of thin pancake mixture. Drop fish into batter, a few pieces at a time, and hold up to drain until no batter appears to remain on fish.

Deep fry in vegetable oil at 375 degrees. Don't let oil overheat. Serve with Tropical Tartar Sauce.

SERVES 6

• •

Secrets: For the Clearwater Fish Fry double recipe.

For the Special Occasion Reception make recipe
4 to 5 times (about 9-pounds grouper) and plan on 100 tiny Parker House rolls.

• •

Frying fish can be messy. Set up a table in the yard
or on the deck. Cover the table with newspapers. Have cookie
sheets or draining racks covered with brown paper bags from the
grocery store, on which to place the fish after frying.

Tropical Tartar Sauce

1   cup mayonnaise
1-2 jalapeño chilies, seeded and minced
2   tablespoons drained, finely chopped
    cornichon pickles
2   tablespoons drained, finely chopped
    capers
2   tablespoons drained, finely chopped
    pitted green olives
2   tablespoons finely chopped fresh cilantro

2   tablespoons chopped fresh chives
1   tablespoon drained, coarsely chopped
    green peppercorns
1-2 tablespoons fresh lime juice
¼   teaspoon grated lime zest
    Salt and freshly ground black pepper,
    to taste
    Cayenne pepper, to taste

Combine all ingredients in a mixing bowl and whisk together until well blended. Correct seasonings, adding salt or lime juice to taste. The mixture should be highly seasoned. Place in an airtight container and refrigerate until needed. This sauce will keep for 1 week.

MAKES 1½ CUPS

Scallop Puffs

3   tablespoons butter
1   pound bay scallops, quartered
2   teaspoons finely minced lemon zest
3   cloves garlic, minced
3   tablespoons chopped fresh dill
2   cups grated Swiss or Gruyère cheese
2   cups good quality mayonnaise

    Freshly ground black pepper
12 dozen 1-inch bread rounds cut from
    good quality white sandwich bread,
    toasted
    Paprika
    Lemon slices and dill sprigs for garnish

Melt butter in a medium skillet over medium-high heat. Add scallops, lemon zest, and garlic. Cook, stirring constantly, 2 to 3 minutes or until the scallops are just barely cooked through. Add dill and cook 30 seconds longer. Let cool to room temperature. Add cheese, mayonnaise, and pepper to the cooled scallop mixture and stir to combine. Cover and refrigerate until ready to use.

Preheat the broiler when ready to bake.

Place toast rounds ½-inch apart on baking sheets. Top each toast round with a heaping teaspoon of the scallop mixture and sprinkle lightly with paprika. Broil the puffs 5-inches from the heat 2 to 3 minutes or until puffed and golden. Transfer puffs to a serving platter and garnish with lemon and dill. Serve hot.

MAKES 12 DOZEN

Scallop Dumplings

These appetizers were a hit at our Pacific Rim Party. They are very easy to
prepare and most impressive to serve. The best secret is to find an Asian market.

2   tablespoons vegetable oil, divided
1   (1-ounce) package fresh chives, cut into
    1-inch pieces
1   green onion, cut into several pieces
1   teaspoon minced fresh ginger
½   pound sea scallops
1   tablespoon plum wine or sherry
2   teaspoons soy sauce

2   teaspoons cornstarch
1   teaspoon Asian sesame oil
½   teaspoon salt
½   teaspoon freshly ground pepper
36 thin wonton skins (round work best)
    Soy-vinegar sauce, orange sweet-and-
    sour sauce, spicy fish sauce (available
    at Asian markets)

Heat 1 tablespoon of the vegetable oil in a skillet. Add the chives, cook and stir over moderately
high heat, until wilted. Transfer to a bowl to cool and set aside.

In a food processor fitted with a steel blade, combine the green onion and ginger and pulse until
the green onion is finely chopped. Add the scallops, plum wine, soy sauce, cornstarch, sesame oil,
salt, and pepper. Pulse until the scallops are finely chopped. Add the reserved chives and pulse just
until evenly incorporated but not smooth.

If using square wonton skins, spread them out on a work surface and cut them with a 3½-inch-round
biscuit cutter. Keep all but 12 skins covered with a damp towel while you proceed. Spoon a heaping
teaspoon of the filling into the center of each wonton skin. Draw the edges up and pleat evenly. Pinch
the pleated edge to form a little bun. Repeat with the remaining wonton skins and filling.

Pour the remaining 1 tablespoon vegetable oil onto a small plate and dip the bottom of each
dumpling in the oil. Arrange the dumplings, without touching, in a bamboo steamer basket. Cover
and steam over boiling water for 10 minutes. Serve with sauces.

MAKES 36 DUMPLINGS

• •

Secret: To make ahead, the cooked dumplings can be refrigerated
for 1 day or frozen for up to 2 weeks. Reheat in a steamer or a
microwave oven. Serve warm with the dipping sauces.

• •

Seafood Lasagna

½ cup butter
2 garlic cloves, crushed
½ cup flour
½ teaspoon salt
2 cups milk
2 cups chicken broth
⅓ cup dry white wine
2 cups shredded mozzarella cheese
½ cup chopped green onions
1 teaspoon basil

1 teaspoon pepper
9 lasagna noodles, oven ready
1 cup cottage cheese, small curd
⅔ cup cooked shrimp, cut in bite-size pieces
⅔ cup cooked bay scallops, cut in bite-size pieces
⅔ cup crabmeat
½ cup Parmesan cheese (optional)

Preheat oven to 350 degrees.

Melt butter in a large saucepan over low heat. Add garlic and cook for 1 minute. Stir in flour and salt. Cook, stirring constantly until bubbly. Remove from heat and stir in milk, broth, and wine. Return to stove and heat to boiling, stirring constantly. Boil for 1 minute. Add mozzarella, onions, basil, and pepper, and cook over low heat until cheese is melted, stirring constantly.

Spread about 1½ cups sauce over the bottom of a 9 x 13-inch ungreased casserole dish and top with 3 lasagna noodles. Spread cottage cheese over noodles. Spread with another 1½ cups sauce and top with 3 more noodles. Spread seafood over this layer and top with another 1½ cups sauce. Cover with the last 3 noodles and top with all the remaining sauce. If desired, top with ½ cup grated Parmesan cheese. Bake uncovered for 35 to 45 minutes or until noodles are tender. Let stand 15 minutes before cutting.

MAKES 9 DINNER SERVINGS, 16 HORS D'OEUVRE SQUARES

• •

Secret: For the Special Occasion Reception make recipe 9 times.

• •

Shrimp Rémoulade

The melange of flavors takes shrimp to a whole new level.

Sauce

¼ cup Creole mustard	½ cup finely chopped parsley
2 tablespoons paprika	½ cup ketchup
1 teaspoon cayenne pepper	½ cup prepared yellow mustard
1 tablespoon salt	2 cloves garlic, minced
1 cup finely chopped green onions	3 eggs (at room temperature)
Dash of Tabasco sauce	Juice of 1 lemon
½ cup finely chopped celery	1⅓ cups salad oil

Shrimp

80 (2½-pounds) medium uncooked shrimp (8 per person), peeled and deveined

Shrimp and crab boil (seasoning mix)
Leaf lettuce

Sauce

Put Creole mustard, paprika, cayenne, salt, green onions, Tabasco, celery, parsley, ketchup, yellow mustard, garlic, eggs, and lemon juice into a blender container. Cover and mix on high speed until well blended. Remove cover and gradually add oil in a steady stream. Sauce will thicken to mayonnaise consistency. Place sauce in an airtight container and refrigerate.

Shrimp

Bring 8 cups of water to a boil in a large pot, add shrimp and crab boil and shrimp. Boil for 2 to 4 minutes or until shrimp turn pink. Drain and rinse with cold water to stop the cooking. Let cool to room temperature, or store in refrigerator until ready to serve. Arrange shrimp on leaf lettuce and top with rémoulade sauce.

SERVES 10

• •
Secret: For the New Orleans Brunch make recipe 3 times.
• •

Shrimp-Sausage Jambalaya

This was so good our guests used spoons to finish off the pot!

4 tablespoons vegetable oil	2½ pounds uncooked medium shrimp,
4 tablespoons flour	peeled and deveined
4 cups chopped onion	2 cups chopped parsley
1 cup chopped green bell pepper	2 cups chopped green onion
1 cup chopped celery	2 cups sliced fresh mushrooms or
½ pound andouille sausage links, sliced or	2 (4½-ounce) jars sliced mushrooms
½ pound smoked sausage links, sliced	⅛ teaspoon cayenne pepper
4½ cups hot water, divided	1 teaspoon garlic powder
¾ cup ketchup	Salt and pepper
	2½ cups long-grain rice, uncooked

In a heavy 5 quart pot, make a roux by combining oil and flour, stirring constantly over low heat until brown or the color of paper bags.

Add onions, bell pepper, and celery and cook and stir constantly until wilted. Add andouille and cook 5 minutes. (Pour in ½ cup of hot water if roux is sticking at this point.) Next, add ketchup, shrimp, parsley, green onions, mushrooms, cayenne, garlic powder, salt, and pepper and stir well.

Add remaining 4 cups water and rice. Bring to a boil, stirring gently. Lower heat and cook covered, for 30 minutes or until rice soaks up the liquid. Stir once or twice during cooking.

SERVES 8 TO 10

● ●

Secret: For the New Orleans Brunch make recipe 3 times.

● ●

Smoked Fish Spread

Spoon spread into Miniature Cream Puffs (see index for recipe) for an impressive hors d'oeuvre.

1 pound (16-ounces) wood smoked fish,	1 bunch green onions, sliced
amberjack or trout	Juice of 2 small lemons
1½ cups (12-ounces) good quality	½ cup (4-ounces) hot sauce
mayonnaise	(Hot Lava Sauce), to taste

Remove skin and bones from fish. Set aside. In a bowl combine mayonnaise, green onions, lemon juice, and hot sauce. Stir until well mixed. Add the fish and mix well. Transfer to an airtight container and refrigerate for at least 1 hour before serving.

MAKES 2 CUPS

Smoked Salmon with Capers, Chopped Red Onion, and Dill-Mustard Sauce

This makes an impressive presentation and is easy to assemble.

Smoked Salmon and Accompaniments

1   loaf (15 slices) high quality
    pumpernickel bread, crusts removed
1   (1½-2 pounds) whole smoked salmon
    fillet (Norwegian or Scottish is best)

Fresh dill sprigs, for garnish
5   lemons, quartered, for garnish
1   cup capers, drained
1   cup finely chopped red onion

Dill-Mustard Sauce

⅓   cup vinegar
7   tablespoons sugar
¼   cups minced fresh dill
1¼ cups Dijon mustard

2   tablespoons ground white pepper
2   tablespoons minced capers
1½ cups extra-virgin olive oil

Whisk together vinegar, sugar, dill, mustard, white pepper, and capers. When well combined, drizzle in the oil while whisking. Whisk until slightly thickened. Cover and refrigerate until ready to use.

MAKES 3 CUPS

Assembly

Cut each bread slice into 4 squares. Place squares on a tray or in a basket for serving. Wash salmon gently with a lemon juice soaked paper towel. Place whole salmon fillet on a large serving platter. Garnish with fresh dill sprigs and lemon quarters. Fill small bowls with capers, chopped red onion, and dill sauce.

SERVES 20 TO 25

● ●

Secret: Have your fish market or specialty food store prepare the smoked salmon.

For the Special Occasion Reception plan on 4 salmon fillets and double the dill-mustard recipe.

● ●

44

Bacon Wrapped Pork Tenderloin

Wrapping the pork with bacon adds another taste dimension, as does the fresh rosemary.

⅔ cup Creole mustard
4 tablespoons ground black pepper
6 tablespoons maple syrup
6 garlic cloves, minced
2 tablespoons chopped fresh rosemary or
　　2 heaping teaspoons dried

3 pounds pork tenderloin
12 slices high quality smoked bacon
12 fresh rosemary sprigs
　　Fresh rosemary sprigs for garnishing

Combine mustard, pepper, maple syrup, garlic, and rosemary in a small bowl. Rub mixture on pork tenderloins, cover and refrigerate 1 hour.

Remove from refrigerator. Wrap 3 bacon slices around each tenderloin (barberpole style) covering completely. Secure with heavy-duty toothpicks. Push rosemary sprigs through each tenderloin.

Prepare fire by piling charcoal or lava rock on 1 side of grill, leaving other side empty. Coat a food rack with vegetable cooking spray, and place on grill. Arrange pork tenderloins over empty side, and grill with lid down, 15 minutes on each side or until a meat thermometer inserted into thickest portion registers 160 degrees. Do not overcook. Pork is safe to eat on the medium side. Remove and discard rosemary sprigs. Cut tenderloins into ½-inch slices. Arrange on platter and garnish with fresh rosemary sprigs.

SERVES 8

Grilled Baby Lamb Chops

2 racks of lamb (cut into 16 chops), ribs
　　Frenched down to the loin meat,
　　lollipop-style
　Olive oil
　Worcestershire sauce

Greek seasoned salt (Cavenders)
Garlic powder
Freshly ground black pepper
Fresh lemon juice

Rub olive oil and Worcestershire into each chop. Sprinkle with Greek seasoning, garlic powder, and pepper, and rub in using your fingers. Let lamb chops sit for 30 to 60 minutes. Grill over hot coals to sear, then reduce heat to medium-low. Cook until medium-rare to medium, about 4 minutes per side. Remove from grill and immediately squeeze lemon juice over chops. Let stand for 10 minutes before serving.

SERVES 4 FOR DINNER AND 8 FOR HORS D'OEUVRES

• •

Secrets: For the Special Occasion Reception serve 300 lamb chops.

To make it easy, have your butcher prepare the chops.

• •

Beef Tenderloin with
Mustard Horseradish Sauce

The little black dress of meats, it's always classic and practically foolproof. Regardless the occasion, or the time of year, you can always build a fabulous menu around beef tenderloin.

1   (4 to 5-pound) whole beef tenderloin, trimmed and tied
Vegetable oil

Freshly ground black pepper
Salt
Mustard Horseradish Sauce (recipe follows)

Remove beef from refrigerator 30 minutes before roasting to bring it to room temperature.

Preheat oven to 500 degrees and position rack in the center.

Rub meat lightly with oil using your hands. Grind black pepper evenly over beef, so that it is well coated. Place beef in a shallow roasting pan. Put into oven, reduce heat to 450 degrees, and roast for 20 to 30 minutes (22 minutes for rare and 25 minutes for medium-rare). Remove from oven, salt meat, cover with aluminum foil, and allow it to rest for 20 minutes. Remove string and slice.

SERVES 8 TO 10 FOR A SEATED DINNER

• •

Secrets: Have your butcher trim and tie the beef tenderloin for you.
This makes your preparation time only a few minutes.

When serving tenderloin buffet style, allow ¼ to ⅓-pound per person.
For a sit-down dinner, allow ½-pound per person.

For the Holiday Cocktail Buffet we recommend using 6 (4 to 5-pound) beef tenderloins.

• •

Mustard Horseradish Sauce

1   cup mayonnaise
1   tablespoon Dijon mustard
1   tablespoon whole-grain mustard

3-4 tablespoons prepared horseradish
½   cup sour cream
¼   teaspoon kosher salt

Whisk together mayonnaise, Dijon mustard, whole-grain mustard, horseradish, sour cream, and kosher salt in a small bowl. Serve at room temperature.

MAKES 1⅔ CUPS

• •

Secret: For the Holiday Cocktail Buffet make recipe 3 times.

• •

Lamb Loins with Mustard Crumbs

Lamb loin, which includes the tenderloin and is often called the saddle,
can be used or the more expensive rib roast is also wonderful with the mustard crumbs.

6 tablespoons unsalted butter plus 10 tablespoons, melted	4 tablespoons coarsely chopped flat-leaf parsley
4 whole boneless lamb loins (about 1 pound each)	4 teaspoons minced garlic
Salt and freshly ground pepper	2 teaspoons minced shallots
½-1 cup all-purpose flour, for dredging	4 teaspoons finely chopped oregano
½ cup plus 4 tablespoons Dijon mustard	4 teaspoons finely chopped basil
2-3 cups coarse dry bread crumbs	4-6 teaspoons freshly grated Parmesan or Romano cheese

Preheat oven to 450 degrees.

Melt 6 tablespoons butter in a large ovenproof skillet. Season lamb loins with salt and pepper and dredge in flour. Add to the skillet and cook over moderately high heat, turning, until browned all over, about 6 minutes. Let the lamb cool slightly, then pat dry and brush with mustard.

In a large bowl, mix bread crumbs with parsley, garlic, shallots, oregano, basil, Parmesan and melted (10 tablespoons) butter. Roll lamb in crumb mixture, pressing it into the meat. Return lamb to the skillet and roast for about 15 minutes for medium-rare meat. Transfer to a cutting surface, and cover loosely with foil and let stand for 5 minutes. Slice the lamb loins ⅓-inch thick and serve.

SERVES 8

• •

Secret: This dish can be made ahead and set aside to be cooked when ready to serve. After rolling lamb in bread crumbs, arrange on a cookie sheet and cover loosely with foil. When about ready to serve, bake as directed in master recipe.

• •

Not-Your-Ordinary Meat Loaf

3	tablespoons unsalted butter		1	teaspoon freshly ground black pepper
¾	cup finely chopped onion		¼	teaspoon cayenne pepper
¾	cup finely chopped green onions		1	teaspoon ground cumin
½	cup finely chopped celery		3	eggs, well beaten
½	cup finely chopped carrots		½	cup ketchup
¼	cup finely minced red bell pepper		½	cup half-and-half
¼	cup finely minced green bell pepper		2	pounds lean ground beef
2	teaspoons minced garlic		12	ounces ground pork
1	teaspoon salt		¼-½	cup fine bread crumbs

Preheat oven to 350 degrees.

Melt butter in a heavy skillet and add onion, green onion, celery, carrots, red and green bell peppers, and garlic. Cook, stirring often, until moisture has evaporated, about 10 minutes. Set aside to cool.

Combine salt, pepper, cayenne, cumin and eggs in a mixing bowl, beat well. Add ketchup and half-and-half. Blend mixture thoroughly.

Add ground beef, ground pork, and bread crumbs to egg mixture. Then add cooled vegetables and mix together with your hands.

Form the mixture into one or two loaves. Place in a baking dish, and place the dish in a larger pan. Pour boiling water into the larger pan until it reaches halfway up the sides of the baking dish. Place in the oven and bake for 50 to 60 minutes.

Remove from water bath. Let stand for 20 minutes before slicing. Add extra ketchup on top of loaf, if desired.

SERVES 8 TO 10

Sticky Ginger Beef with Rice

Beef

5	green onions, halved crosswise (for garnish)
2½	pounds lean beef, cut into strips
¼	cup sugar

3¾	cups basmati rice
18-20	saffron threads
1	tablespoon boiling water
¼	cup toasted sesame oil

Sauce

¾	cup white wine vinegar
1¼	cups hoisin sauce
1	tablespoon Worcestershire sauce
	A few drops Tabasco sauce

4	small pieces pickled ginger, finely chopped
	Salt and pepper, to taste

Beef

Cut green onions into long thin strips and put them in a bowl of ice water for about 20 minutes to crisp and curl.

Coat the beef with sugar and set aside.

Wash rice in several changes of water and drain well. Mix saffron with the boiling water and let stand for 10 minutes. Boil rice and saffron in a large pan of salted water for 8 to 10 minutes or until the rice is soft outside but firm inside. Drain, cover with foil, and keep warm.

Heat some of the sesame oil in a wok or heavy frying pan. Stir-fry the beef in batches for 3 to 5 minutes or until brown. Transfer each cooked batch to a plate.

Sauce

Add vinegar to the wok and simmer over high heat until reduced to about ¼ cup. Lower heat to medium and add hoisin, Worcestershire, Tabasco, and chopped ginger. Season to taste with salt and pepper. When the sauce starts to bubble, add beef and heat through for 2 to 3 minutes.

To serve, drain and dry green onions. Spoon hot rice and beef into separate serving dishes and garnish with green onions.

SERVES 10 TO 12

• •

Secrets: For advance preparation, chop the ginger up to 2 days before, cover and keep cool. Cut the green onions, place in ice water, cover and refrigerate. Slice the beef, cover and refrigerate up to 1 day ahead.

For the Pacific Rim Dinner we recommend omitting the rice.

• •

Pork Tenderloin Medallions with Apple Relish

Marinade
4   tablespoons dry mustard
4   teaspoons whole thyme leaves
1   cup dry sherry
1   cup soy sauce

4   garlic cloves, minced
1   teaspoon ground ginger
4-5 pounds pork tenderloin

Apple Relish
1   (8-ounce) package cream cheese, softened
½   cup sour cream
2   tablespoons prepared horseradish,
     drained slightly

2   Granny Smith apples, peeled, chopped
     fine and rinsed with lemon juice

Garnish
4   cups chutney, chopped and drained
2   (2-ounce) jars diced pimento

2   bunches parsley, washed and stems
     removed

Marinating and Roasting Pork
Combine dry mustard, thyme, sherry, soy sauce, garlic, and ginger in a large zip-top plastic bag. Add pork and marinate overnight in the refrigerator.

Preheat oven to 325 degrees when ready to cook.

Remove pork from marinade, pat dry, and place in a roasting pan. Bake, uncovered, for approximately 1 hour or until internal temperature registers 160-165 degrees on a meat thermometer. Remove meat from oven and cool. Do not overcook. Pork is safe to eat on the medium to medium-rare side.

Apple Relish
While pork is roasting, combine cream cheese and sour cream, mixing until smooth. Add horseradish and mix in chopped apple. Set aside.

Assembly and Garnish
Cut cooled pork tenderloins into ¼-inch slices. Dab each slice with about ½ teaspoon of chopped, drained chutney and top this with a scant ¼ teaspoon of Apple Relish. Garnish with a small square of drained pimento and a tiny parsley leaf.

SERVES 50

• •

Secret: We adapted the pork recipe to this use, but is really marvelous served warm as a main dish with a delicious sauce made by combining 1 (10-ounce) jar apricot preserves, 1 tablespoon soy sauce and 2 tablespoons dry sherry. Heat ingredients in a saucepan until well blended.

• •

The Pork Tenderloin Medallions with Apple Relish was a very popular recipe at the daytime Silver Coffee. We figured on 100 individual servings, or 30 inches of meat. Two batches of apple relish are required. For a Friday morning party, the meat is generally put into the marinade on Tuesday evening and cooked early the next day. The roast is sliced on Wednesday afternoon and the medallions are assembled the day before the party. Any kind of chutney is good, but we prefer a mango chutney. We whirl this relish in a food processor fitted with the steel blade for just a minute or so, then allow it to drain by spreading it over a strainer lined with folded paper towels. We found measuring spoons to be cumbersome when dolloping. We prefer to use thin, long handled baby food spoons.

Grilled Flank Steak

The flank is a thin but flavorful steak and is easy on the purse strings.

2   (1½ to 2-pound) flank steaks

Marinade

½ cup soy sauce
2   tablespoons olive oil (may omit oil)

2   teaspoons dried thyme
2   teaspoons ground black pepper

Score steaks across top with a sharp knife. Combine soy sauce, olive oil, thyme, and pepper in a shallow baking dish. Add steak and turn to coat with marinade. Cover and refrigerate 3 to 6 hours or overnight.

Prepare the barbeque grill (high heat) or preheat the broiler. Grill or broil steak over high heat, 3 inches from the heat source, 4 minutes per side for medium-rare. Remove to a cutting board and let rest for 10 minutes before slicing. Thinly slice steak on the diagonal (across the grain) and arrange on a platter. Pour meat juices over steak and serve.

SERVES 10

• •

Secret: Watch the broiling or grilling time carefully so the meat doesn't overcook.

• •

Five-Spice Chicken Salad in Wonton Cups

Asian-flavored chicken salad is served in simple baked wonton cups.
This is a wonderful recipe for entertaining because everything can be made ahead.

Wonton Shells

48 wonton wrappers   Butter-flavored cooking spray

Chicken Salad

2   teaspoons five-spice powder   1   large shallot, minced
    (available in the spice section of   1   tablespoon fresh orange juice
    most grocery stores)   1   tablespoon rice vinegar
1½ teaspoons salt   1   tablespoon honey
1   large whole skinless, boneless chicken   1   tablespoon olive oil
    breast   ¼   cup finely chopped fresh cilantro
1   medium navel orange   Fresh cilantro leaves

Wonton Shells

Preheat oven to 350 degrees.

Trim the wonton wrappers to form 2-inch squares. Coat mini-muffin pans with cooking spray and press a wonton square into each cup. Lightly spray with cooking spray and bake for about 7 minutes, or until lightly browned. Let cool in the pan. The wonton cups can be stored in an airtight container at room temperature for up to a week.

Chicken Salad

Preheat oven to 350 degrees.

In a small bowl, combine the five-spice powder and salt and sprinkle on both sides of the chicken. Transfer to an oiled baking sheet and bake for about 18 minutes, or until cooked through. Let the chicken cool and cut into ¼-inch pieces.

Using a vegetable peeler, remove zest from half the orange (leave behind the bitter white pith). Cut the zest into very thin 1-inch-long strips. Measure 1 packed teaspoon of zest, set aside and reserve the rest. Peel the rest of the orange and divide into sections. Cut the sections into ¼-inch pieces.

In a medium bowl, combine orange pieces, shallot, orange juice, rice vinegar, honey, and olive oil. Gently stir in chicken, 1 teaspoon orange zest, and cilantro. The chicken salad can be made 1 day ahead. Store in an airtight container in the refrigerator.

Assembly

Spoon 2 teaspoons chicken salad into each wonton cup. Garnish with reserved orange zest and tiny cilantro leaves and serve.

MAKES 48

• •

Secret: Wonton wrappers are available in the produce department of most grocery stores. These little baked cups are useful containers for all kinds of hot or cold savory fillings.

• •

Lemon Chicken

Decadently delicious, surprisingly sweet!

2 chickens (2½-pounds each) cut into quarters	½ cup corn oil
2 cups fresh lemon juice	2 tablespoons grated lemon zest
2 cups flour	¼ cup brown sugar
2 teaspoons salt	¼ cup chicken stock
2 teaspoons paprika	1 teaspoon lemon extract
1 teaspoon ground black pepper	2 lemons, sliced paper thin

Combine chicken pieces and lemon juice in a bowl just large enough to hold them comfortably. Cover and marinate in the refrigerator a few hours, turning occasionally.

Drain chicken thoroughly and pat dry. Fill a plastic bag with flour, salt, paprika, and black pepper, and shake well to mix. Put 2 pieces of chicken into the bag at a time and shake, coating completely.

Preheat oven to 350 degrees.

Heat corn oil in a frying pan or cast-iron Dutch oven until hot and fry chicken pieces, a few at a time, until well browned and crisp. This will take about 10 minutes per batch.

Arrange browned chicken in a single layer in a large shallow baking pan. Sprinkle evenly with lemon zest and brown sugar. Mix chicken stock and lemon extract together and pour around chicken pieces. Set a thin lemon slice on top of each piece of chicken. Bake chicken for 35 to 40 minutes or until tender. The chicken is good served hot or at room temperature.

SERVES 8

• •

Secret: May be made one day ahead. Prepare chicken up to the baking step. Instead of baking, cover and refrigerate. Do the final baking timed to finish just before the party begins.

• •

If you are having a large party, use chicken drumettes or boneless chicken breasts, sliced into tenders, instead of chicken quarters. They make great appetizers.

Sticky Red Curry Chicken Wings

½ cup palm sugar or dark brown sugar
½ cup tomato paste
¼ cup Thai red curry paste

2   teaspoons salt
10 chicken drumettes (wings with tips cut off)
    Vegetable oil for greasing

Heat brown sugar and tomato paste in a pan over low heat for 4 to 5 minutes or until the sugar has dissolved. Remove from the heat, stir in the curry paste and salt and let cool.

Pour the cooled marinade over the chicken wings and toss well to coat. Place wings in a freezer strength zip-top plastic bag, which can be turned for even coating. Marinate in the refrigerator for at least 4 hours.

Preheat oven to 375 degrees when ready to roast.

Transfer marinated wings to a lightly oiled roasting pan and spread them out. Roast wings for 35 to 40 minutes or until cooked and slightly charred.

MAKES 10 CHICKEN WINGS

• •

Secrets: Cook, cover, and refrigerate the chicken wings up to
1 day ahead. If serving the wings hot, reheat at 375 degrees for 20 minutes,
or until piping hot. Don't make wings too saucy or they'll be too messy to eat.

For the Pacific Rim Dinner double recipe.

• •

> **F**or dressier parties, we recommend using chicken
> tenders on a skewer. They are not as messy to eat. Make sure when
> roasting the tenders that you cover them with foil for the first
> 15 minutes. Uncover and continue roasting until done.
> Do not overcook, as they will dry out.

Black Bread with
Goat Cheese and Sun-Dried Tomatoes

2   loaves (15 slices per loaf) good quality
    pumpernickel bread
1   (2-ounce) package sun-dried tomatoes,
    softened according to package
    directions

2   (8-ounce) packages cream cheese
2   (4-ounce) packages feta cheese
½   pound (2 sticks) unsalted butter
2   packages small basil leaves

Preheat oven to 350 degrees.

Use a 1½-inch round cutter to cut pumpernickel into rounds, 4 rounds per slice. Toast rounds in oven just until crisp. Remove and set aside.

Drain and pat dry tomatoes. Cut tomatoes into ⅛-inch slices. Process cream cheese, feta cheese, and butter in a food processor fitted with the steel blade until well blended.

To assemble, spread each round generously with cheese mixture, top with a slice of sun-dried tomato, and garnish with a basil leaf.

MAKES 120

• •

Secret: All ingredients may be prepared a day ahead. Store toast rounds in zip-top plastic bags. Store cheese mixture in an airtight container in the refrigerator. When ready to assemble, bring cheese mixture to room temperature and assemble as in master recipe.

• •

Chicken Salad Tea Sandwiches with Smoked Almonds

6   cups chicken broth or water
4   whole (about 3 pounds) boneless
    chicken breasts with skin, halved
2   cups mayonnaise, divided
⅔   cup minced shallots
2   teaspoons fresh tarragon leaves, minced

Salt and pepper
48 pieces high quality white bread, thinly
    sliced
1   cup (4-ounces) smoked almonds, finely
    chopped

In a deep 12-inch skillet bring broth or water to a boil and add chicken breasts in one layer. Reduce heat and poach chicken at a low simmer, turning once (about 7 minutes). Remove skillet from heat and cool chicken in cooking liquid 20 minutes. Discard skin and finely shred chicken. In a bowl stir together chicken, 1 cup mayonnaise, shallots, tarragon, salt, and pepper to taste. Refrigerate until ready to use.

When ready to prepare sandwiches, spread chicken salad on half the slices of bread and cover with remaining slices, pressing together gently. Trim off the crusts. Cut each sandwich on the diagonal making 4 triangles. Sandwiches may be made ahead to this point. Cover with a damp cloth, wrap tightly in plastic wrap, and refrigerate overnight.

To prepare for serving, put chopped almonds on a small plate and spread one short edge of each sandwich triangle with remaining mayonnaise, coating well. Dip coated edge in the almonds. Wrap in plastic wrap and chill until ready to serve.

MAKES 96 SANDWICHES

• •

Secret: If you have a time crunch, purchase 3 pounds of rotisserie chicken
instead of cooking your own. You can use just the white meat or both white and dark.

• •

Cucumber Tea Sandwiches

*This zesty concoction, served at many Coffees in
the early years has proven itself to be an enduring favorite.*

1 loaf thin-sliced good quality pumpernickel bread	3 ounces mayonnaise
1 small white onion, peeled	3 (3-ounce) packages cream cheese, softened
2 cucumbers, peeled and seeded	Seasoned salt (Jane's Krazy Mixed-Up Salt)
1 clove garlic	

Use a 2-inch round cutter to cut pumpernickel into rounds (4 rounds per slice).

Chop onion, cucumbers, and garlic together in a food processor fitted with the steel blade. Scrape this mixture into a strainer lined with paper towels and allow to drain well, 15 minutes or more, then squeeze out the extra liquid. Combine mayonnaise, cream cheese, and seasoned salt in a large bowl and mix until of spreading consistency. Stir in the drained, chopped vegetables.

To assemble, spread each round with cucumber mixture and top with another round.

MAKES ABOUT 60

• •

Secret: Over the years we have used a variety of breads and fillings
for tea sandwiches. Some have been open-faced with elaborate garnishes; others
have been closed and cut into a number of shapes. Despite the differences, certain common
elements exist. We try to slice our breads as thinly as possible and to make the sandwiches
bite-sized. Freshness is essential, because thinly sliced bread becomes stale very quickly.
Accordingly, we make small batches, and keep dampened tea towels at hand to place over
completed sandwiches, which are stored in the refrigerator as they are made.

• •

For the Coffee, we would make about 100 of these sandwiches.
This requires about 2 loaves of bread for open-faced sandwiches and
about 1½ batches of filling. We make the filling two days in advance of
the party to allow the flavors to meld together. Fancy open-faced sandwiches
are assembled at the last minute on party day, but those made with 2 slices
of bread can be put together the day before. Store in the refrigerator
covered with damp paper towels and wrapped tightly with plastic wrap.

Mini Bacon, Lettuce and Tomato Tea Sandwiches

2 loaves high quality white bread, thinly sliced (Pepperidge Farm)	24 Roma tomatoes
Unsalted butter, softened	Salt and pepper
Mayonnaise	48 slices cooked bacon
	2-3 heads butter lettuce

Lightly butter each slice of bread. Add a thin layer of mayonnaise to half the buttered slices. Make a sandwich out of the bread using one buttered slice and one butter with mayonnaise slice. Use a 1-inch round cutter and cut 4 rounds out of each sandwich. Cover with a damp towel. If not using immediately, cover with plastic wrap and refrigerate.

Slice tomatoes ¼-inch thick. Drain tomatoes on paper towels. Sprinkle with salt and pepper. Cut bacon into 1-inch pieces. Tear lettuce into 1-inch pieces. Place a piece of bacon and a piece of lettuce on each slice of tomato. If not using immediately, cover with plastic wrap and refrigerate. The sandwiches may be made ahead until this point and refrigerated overnight.

When ready to serve the sandwiches, bring bread and tomatoes to room temperature. Peel bread apart, add dressed tomato slices and remake the sandwich.

MAKES 48 SANDWICHES

Open-Faced Cucumber Sandwiches

Even people who don't like cucumbers love these!

1 loaf good quality white bread (Pepperidge Farm)	Mayonnaise (may use light variety)
2 cucumbers, scored and thinly sliced	Seasoned salt (Jane's Krazy Mixed-Up Salt)
	Dried dill weed

Prepare the bread by cutting the crusts off and slicing into fourths. You will have 4 small squares per slice. Spread a generous amount of mayonnaise on each slice. Top with a cucumber slice and sprinkle liberally with seasoned salt and a small amount of dill weed. Cover with a damp paper towel and store in the refrigerator until ready to serve.

MAKES ABOUT 80

• •

Secret: Although the bread can be sliced ahead of time, it's best to add the cucumbers just before serving.

• •

Smoked Turkey Breast on Tiny Orange Muffins

½ pound smoked turkey breast, shaved (purchase at a meat market or delicatessen)

¾ cup hot pepper jelly or garlic marmalade

2 heads butter or baby Bibb lettuce, washed and dried

30 orange muffins

Orange Muffins

1½ cups granulated sugar, divided

½ cup unsalted butter, at room temperature

2 eggs

1 teaspoon baking soda

1 cup buttermilk

2 cups sifted all-purpose flour

½ teaspoon salt

1 cup raisins

Zest 1 orange

Juice of 1 orange

Preheat oven to 400 degrees.

Butter miniature muffin pans. In a large bowl, using an electric mixer, beat together 1 cup sugar and butter until smooth and creamy. Add eggs and beat until fluffy.

In a small bowl, combine baking soda and buttermilk. In another bowl sift flour and salt together. With the mixer on low speed, add the flour mixture to the butter mixture alternating with the buttermilk and soda combination, beginning and ending with the dry ingredients. Stir until well mixed.

In a food processor fitted with the steel blade, grind together raisins and orange zest. Add to batter and mix well. Spoon or pipe batter into prepared muffin pans. Fill muffin cups about ⅔ full.

Bake 12 minutes or until golden brown and firm to the touch. Remove from oven and set muffin pans close together on a wire rack. While still warm, brush tops of muffins with orange juice and sprinkle with remaining ½ cup sugar. Remove muffins from cups after 5 minutes and allow to cool completely.

Assembly

Cut each muffin in half crosswise. Mound shaved turkey on each muffin bottom. Spread the turkey with ½ teaspoon jelly or marmalade and top with a piece of lettuce allowing edges to show. Cover with the muffin top.

MAKES 30 MINIATURE MUFFINS

● ●

Secret: For the Southern Silver Coffee make recipe four times.

● ●

Artichokes and Roasted Peppers in Toast Cups

Artichoke Mixture

2 tablespoons unsalted butter
1 bunch green onions, trimmed and
      minced
2 cloves garlic, minced
1 can (13¾-ounces) artichoke bottoms,
      drained and cut into ¼-inch pieces
3 ounces thinly sliced prosciutto, minced

3 tablespoons finely shredded basil leaves
⅔ cup (2-ounces) grated Parmesan cheese
½ cup (2-ounces) grated Jarlsberg or
      Gruyère cheese
1 tablespoon fresh lemon juice
      Freshly ground black pepper, to taste
½ cup good mayonnaise

Roasted Peppers

3 red bell peppers
3 yellow bell peppers
¼ cup olive oil
2 tablespoons balsamic vinegar

   Salt, to taste
48 toast cups (see index for recipe or may
      use purchased frozen phyllo cups or
      small pastry cups)

Artichoke Mixture

Melt butter in a small skillet over medium-high heat. Add green onions and garlic and cook, stirring frequently, for 2 to 3 minutes, or just until softened. Transfer to a medium-size mixing bowl. Add artichoke bottoms, prosciutto, basil, Parmesan, and Jarlsberg to the green onions and toss to combine. Sprinkle with lemon juice and pepper. Stir mayonnaise into this mixture and refrigerate at least one hour.

Roasted Peppers

Preheat oven to 400 degrees.

Stem and seed each pepper, then cut into 1-inch square chunks. Place peppers in a single layer in a large, shallow baking dish. Drizzle with olive oil and vinegar and sprinkle with salt and pepper. Roast peppers 15 minutes, stirring once halfway through the cooking time. Remove from oven and let cool.

Assembly

Preheat broiler.

Place a pepper piece into the bottom of each toast cup and mound 2 teaspoons of the artichoke mixture onto each pepper piece. Arrange the cups in rows on baking sheets and broil 3 to 4 inches from the heat until puffed and bubbly, about 2 minutes. Allow to cool for a few minutes and transfer to a serving tray.

MAKES 48

Mushroom, Walnut, and Gruyère Strudel Rolls

*These crowd pleasers make up very quickly and may
be frozen ahead. Pop them in the oven when time is of the essence.*

Mushroom, Walnut, Gruyère Filling

3 tablespoons butter	½ cup finely chopped green onions
2 tablespoons finely chopped shallots	⅓ cup minced parsley
1 pound mushrooms, chopped	1 tablespoon lemon juice
1 teaspoon salt	1½ cups walnuts, lightly toasted and finely
1 teaspoon pepper	chopped
½ cup dry white wine	½ pound (8-ounces) Gruyère cheese, grated

Strudel Rolls

16 sheets phyllo dough, thawed (half of 16-ounce package)	½ cup (1 stick) butter, melted

Mushroom, Walnut, Gruyère Filling

Melt butter in a medium skillet over medium heat. Add shallots, mushrooms, salt, and pepper, and cook over medium heat until most of the liquid has evaporated. Add wine and cook until evaporated, stirring constantly. Remove from the heat and put in a bowl. Stir in green onion, parsley, and lemon juice. Let cool, then add the walnuts and cheese. Blend thoroughly. You may make the filling a day ahead. Cover bowl and refrigerate.

Assembly

Preheat oven to 375 degrees.

When working with phyllo, it is important to keep unused dough covered with plastic wrap and a damp towel until you are ready to use. For each strudel roll, lay out 1 full sheet of phyllo on plastic wrap, brush it lightly with butter, top with a second sheet and butter again. Do this 2 more times for a total of 4 sheets.

Spread ¼ of the filling along one of the longer sides of the phyllo and roll up as you would a jelly-roll, tucking in the ends as you go, using the plastic wrap to help you. Set the rolls on a buttered jelly-roll pan seam sides down. Repeat using the remaining 12 sheets of phyllo for a total of 4 strudel rolls.

Brush the rolls with a little butter and lightly score them into bite-size pieces with a sharp knife. Bake for 25 minutes or until golden. Let stand for 5 minutes before slicing.

MAKES 64

• •

Secrets: For the Cool Weather Warm Hearth Supper you only need half this recipe.

These may be frozen. Defrost before baking as directed.

You can find phyllo dough in the frozen food section of the grocery store.

Spray butter makes easy work of buttering pastry sheets.

• •

Crudités - Vegetables For Dipping with Anchovy Mayonnaise and Curry Honey Sauce

Vegetables used for crudités benefit from a quick immersion in rapidly boiling salted water, or blanching. Blanching maximizes their flavor and color and makes them tender yet crispy. Vegetables require varying amounts of blanching time.

Vegetables

Cauliflower, asparagus, Green beans, broccoli, carrots, snow peas, Brussels sprouts
Anchovy Mayonnaise and Curry Honey Sauce (recipes follow)

General Blanching Directions

Trim or peel vegetables if necessary, and cut asparagus into equal lengths. Prepare a large bowl of ice water. Blanch a small quantity of each vegetable in boiling water. Immediately immerse in ice-cold water to stop cooking and chill vegetables. Drain well and pat dry with paper towels if wet. Store on racks placed on paper toweling. Cover with paper towels. Wrap in plastic and refrigerate until ready to use.

Cauliflower

5 to 6 minutes.

Asparagus

3 to 5 minutes, depending on thickness of stalk.

Green Beans

2 to 4 minutes, depending on freshness and size.

Broccoli

Approximately 3 minutes to tenderize and brighten color.

Carrots

Approximately 3 minutes to brighten color.

Snow Peas

Approximately 30 seconds.

Brussels Sprouts

Approximately 8 minutes to tenderize.

● ●
Secret: Do not put too many vegetables in boiling water at one time.
● ●

Anchovy Mayonnaise

1	pint (16-ounces) good quality mayonnaise	2	hard-boiled egg yolks, sieved or diced
4-5	oil packed anchovy fillets, finely chopped	¼	cup minced parsley
1	large garlic clove, minced	1½	tablespoons capers, drained and minced
			Pinch cayenne pepper (optional)

Mix mayonnaise, anchovies, garlic, egg yolks, parsley, and capers, together until blended. Then add cayenne, if desired. Store in an airtight container and refrigerate until ready to use.

MAKES 1 PINT

Curry Honey Sauce

1 cup honey
3 tablespoons curry powder

1 cup good mayonnaise

Pour honey into saucepan and heat. Bring to a boil and stir in curry. Remove from heat and blend with mayonnaise. Store in an airtight container and refrigerate at least overnight. The sauce will thicken as it cools.

MAKES 1½ CUPS

• •

Secrets: Serve with carrots, peapods, or other vegetables.
It is also good with cubes of melon and pineapple.

This dip keeps for weeks in the refrigerator.

• •

Steamed Fresh Asparagus with Tomato-Basil Dip or Mill's Mayonnaise

2 pounds fresh asparagus
   Tomato-Basil Dip or Mill's Mayonnaise (recipes follow)

Cut off tough ends of asparagus and make them uniform in length (about 4 to 6-inches). Remove scales with a vegetable peeler, if desired. Prepare the ice bath by filling a large bowl with water and lots of ice. Cook asparagus in a large pot of boiling water until crisp-tender, about 3 minutes. Drain and immediately plunge into ice water to stop the cooking process, drain and pat dry. Wrap in paper towels, place in a zip-top plastic bag, and refrigerate until ready to serve. When ready to serve, arrange asparagus on a serving platter along with bowls of the Tomato-Basil Dip or Mill's Mayonnaise.

SERVES 8 TO 10

• •

Secrets: Immediately plunging the asparagus into the ice water turns them bright green.

For the Southern Silver Coffee use 8 to 10 pounds of asparagus and Mill's Mayonnaise.

• •

Tomato-Basil Dip

This dip is so good even picky eaters will eat their vegetables.

1 cup mayonnaise
½ cup sour cream
1 tablespoon tomato paste

½ cup chopped fresh basil
1 tablespoon grated lemon rind

Whisk together mayonnaise, sour cream, tomato paste, fresh basil, and lemon rind until blended. Store in an airtight container and refrigerate until needed.

MAKES ABOUT 1½ CUPS

• •

Secrets: This is a beautiful, fresh-tasting dip which also tastes great with red and yellow bell pepper strips. Don't skip anything, especially the fresh basil and lemon rind. This dip keeps well in the refrigerator for several days and is nice to have on hand for impromptu entertaining.

• •

Mill's Mayonnaise

3 teaspoons dry mustard
3 teaspoons paprika

Juice of 3 lemons
   (approximately 6 tablespoons)
3 cups good mayonnaise

Mix dry mustard and paprika in lemon juice to make a thin paste. Add to mayonnaise and mix well. Store in an airtight container and refrigerate until ready to serve.

MAKES ABOUT 3 CUPS

Roasted Eggplant Spread with Pita Crisps

There is very little fat in this spread so you can save your calories for dessert.

1 medium eggplant (about 1 pound), peeled
2 red bell peppers, seeded
1 red onion, peeled
2 garlic cloves, minced

3 tablespoons good olive oil
1½ teaspoons kosher salt
½ teaspoon ground pepper
1 tablespoon tomato paste
   Pita Crisps

Preheat oven to 400 degrees.

Cut eggplant, bell peppers, and onion into 1-inch pieces. Toss vegetables in a large bowl with garlic, olive oil, salt, and pepper. Spread mixture on a baking sheet. Roast for 45 minutes or until the vegetables are lightly browned and soft, tossing once during cooking. Cool slightly.

Place vegetables in a food processor fitted with a steel blade, add tomato paste. Using on and off turns, process until coarse purée forms. Place in an airtight container, cover, and refrigerate until ready to use. Bring to room temperature 1 hour before serving. Can be made 1 day ahead.

MAKES ABOUT 2 CUPS

Pita Crisps

6 (7- to 8-inch) diameter pita breads, each cut into 8 triangles

3 tablespoons olive oil

Preheat oven to 450 degrees.

Place pita triangles in a large bowl. Drizzle with oil and toss to coat. Arrange on a baking sheet in a single layer. Sprinkle with salt and pepper. Bake about 7 minutes or until crisp and golden. Cool completely. Store in an airtight container at room temperature. They are best made 8 hours ahead.

MAKES 48

Spinach and Artichoke Pinwheels

1 (17.3-ounce) package frozen puff pastry
1 (10-ounce) package frozen chopped
   spinach, thawed
1 (14-ounce) can artichoke hearts, drained
   and chopped

½ cup mayonnaise
½ cup grated Parmesan cheese
1 teaspoon onion powder
1 teaspoon garlic powder
½ teaspoon pepper

Thaw puff pastry at room temperature 30 minutes.

Drain spinach well, pressing between layers of paper towels. Stir together spinach, artichoke hearts, mayonnaise, Parmesan, onion powder, garlic powder, and pepper.

Unfold thawed pastry, and place on a lightly floured surface or heavy-duty plastic wrap. Spread one-half spinach mixture evenly over pastry sheet, leaving a ½-inch border. Roll up pastry, jelly-roll fashion, pressing to seal seam. Wrap in heavy-duty plastic wrap. Repeat procedure with remaining pastry and spinach mixture. Freeze 30 minutes.

Preheat oven to 400 degrees.

Remove from freezer and cut into ½-inch-thick slices. Bake for 20 minutes or until golden brown. (Rolls may be frozen up to 3 months.)

MAKES 4 DOZEN

Try substituting the filling ingredients with 4-ounces thinly sliced prosciutto, ¾ cup (packed) grated Gruyère cheese (about 2½-ounces), and 2 tablespoons chopped fresh basil. Prepare the pastry the same way. Arrange prosciutto over pastry sheet, leaving ½-inch border along one side. Sprinkle prosciutto with half of basil, then top with half of cheese. Continue with the directions in the master recipe.

Spinach Cakes

You will learn to love these humble cakes for their versatility and flavor.

4   tablespoons (½ stick) butter
½   cup flour, divided
½   cup chopped onions
1   cup milk
4   cups (about 6-ounces) clean organic
      baby spinach
1¼ teaspoons salt
⅛   teaspoon cayenne pepper
¼   teaspoon ground white pepper

¼   teaspoon grated nutmeg
2   teaspoons chopped garlic
½   cup dried fine bread crumbs
2   tablespoons freshly grated Parmesan
      cheese
1   tablespoon Pernod (licorice flavored
      liqueur)
¼   cup vegetable oil
2   teaspoons Creole seasoning

Heat butter in a skillet over medium-high heat. Add ¼ cup flour and stir constantly for about 5 to 6 minutes. Make a blond roux, the color of sandpaper.

Add onions and cook, stirring for about 2 minutes or until slightly wilted. Add milk and stir until mixture thickens, 3 to 4 minutes. Add spinach, salt, cayenne, white pepper, nutmeg, and garlic and cook, stirring for about 4 minutes. Remove from heat. Add bread crumbs, Parmesan, and Pernod and mix well. Let cool for about 30 minutes.

Divide mixture into 4 equal portions and shape into patties. Heat oil in a nonstick skillet over medium-high heat. Combine remaining ¼ cup flour and Creole seasoning. Dredge patties, coating evenly, in flour. Fry the cakes for about 1½ minutes on each side or until golden. Transfer to a platter and keep warm until ready to serve.

MAKES 4 MAIN COURSE CAKES

• •

Secrets: Triple this recipe to make 50 (1½-inch) bite-size spinach
cakes to use for hors d'oeuvres, especially to balance meats and seafood offerings.

These cakes can be reheated by placing them on
a baking sheet in a 400 degree oven for 4 to 5 minutes.

For the Book Club Luncheon make recipe 3 times to make 12 main course servings.

• •

Steamed New Potatoes with Chive Butter

*An inspiration of one Silver Sister, this recipe is one of our
all time favorites. It was quite a novelty at the time is was introduced, and the
creamy, rich filling with its tang of salt and chive remains a classic.*

4   (8-ounce) packages cream cheese,
     softened
1   pound (4 sticks) lightly salted butter,
     softened
4   tablespoons minced chives
1   teaspoon garlic powder

1   teaspoon white pepper
1   teaspoon seasoned salt
     (Jane's Krazy Mixed-Up Salt)
48 new potatoes, the size of a 50 cent
     piece, washed but unpeeled
     Fresh parsley, for garnish

Blend together cream cheese, butter, chives, garlic powder, white pepper, and salt until smooth in a food processor fitted with the steel blade. The mixture should taste somewhat salty. Cover and refrigerate the filling.

Cook the potatoes, 16 at a time, in a microwave oven on high for about 15 minutes. To make sure the potatoes cook evenly, arrange the potatoes on paper towels in a large single circle around the perimeter of the microwave. Cover with additional paper towels. Cook for 5 minutes. Give potatoes a half turn and cook 5 minutes more. Check for doneness. They should be firm and slightly harder than you would normally serve them. (The amount of cooking time will vary with the size of the potatoes and the individual microwave oven.)

Allow potatoes to cool completely and cut them into halves. Using the smaller end of a melon baller, scoop out a ¼-inch deep depression from the cut side of each potato. Fill the depression with the prepared filling, mounding it to cover the entire top of the potato. (You may need to trim a sliver from the bottom of some of the potato halves in order to keep them from wobbling.) If desired, fit a pastry bag with a fluted tip and fill with softened filling. Pipe a wreath around the edge of each potato, finishing with a small rosette in the center. However, be careful to not use too much of the butter mixture, or they will be too rich. Garnish by placing a tiny parsley leaf in the middle of each rosette. Cover and refrigerate until ready to serve.

MAKES 96

• •

Secrets: This easy-to-make filling can be prepared several days in advance.
Cook the potatoes and fill and garnish them the day before serving.

Take time when selecting potatoes. It is important that they be the same small size.

• •

In order to insure professional results, the process of cutting the potatoes in half should be done carefully. An ultra sharp knife will keep the fragile potato skins from tearing. Practice will make the cuts straight and judicious filling will camouflage the ones that slant.

Tomato Tartlets

Tomato Sauce

3   tablespoons olive oil
½   cup chopped onion
4   garlic cloves, minced

1   (28-ounce) can chopped tomatoes
     (do not drain)
3   fresh sage leaves
1   fresh rosemary sprig

Tartlets

1   (17¼-ounce) package frozen puff pastry,
     thawed
½   cup grated mozzarella cheese
6   plum tomatoes, sliced into ⅛-inch rounds

⅓   cup olive oil
     Salt
     Freshly ground black pepper
2   tablespoons minced fresh basil

Tomato Sauce

Heat 3 tablespoons oil in heavy medium skillet over medium heat. Add onion and garlic and sauté until translucent, about 5 minutes. Add chopped tomatoes, sage, and rosemary to the skillet. Simmer tomato mixture until reduced to 1½ cups thick purée, about 30 minutes. Set aside. May be made a day ahead. Cover and refrigerate.

Tartlets

Preheat oven to 425 degrees.

Roll out puff pastry sheet to thickness of ⅛-inch. Using a 5-inch diameter plate as guide, cut out 4 pastry rounds. Repeat with remaining pastry sheet, forming a total of 8 rounds. Place 4 rounds on each of 2 baking sheets.

Bring tomato sauce to room temperature and spread a generous 2 tablespoons tomato purée over each round, leaving ½-inch borders. Sprinkle with 1 tablespoon mozzarella. Arrange sliced tomato rounds over cheese. Bake for about 15 minutes, or until tarts are golden brown.

Remove from oven and drizzle a small amount of olive oil over tarts and season with salt and pepper. Sprinkle fresh basil over each tart and serve. May be served at room temperature.

MAKES 8 TARTS OR CUT THEM INTO FOURTHS TO SERVE AS APPETIZERS

• •

Secret: For the Sip and See double recipe and cut each tartlet into fourths.

• •

Hot Cheese Bites

The first time we served these bites at a Silver Coffee Party,
they disappeared. We made twice as many for the next party with the same result.

2   cups (8-ounces) sharp Cheddar cheese, grated
½   cup (2-ounces) slivered almonds
6   slices bacon, cooked and crumbled
1   small onion, grated

1   teaspoon Worcestershire sauce
1   (8-ounce) jar good mayonnaise
½   loaf good quality white bread (Pepperidge Farm)

Preheat oven to 400 degrees.

Mix together cheese, almonds, bacon, onion, Worcestershire, and mayonnaise. Remove crusts from bread and cut each slice into 4 triangles or squares. Spread one side of each triangle with cheese mixture. Place on cookie sheets and bake for 10 minutes or until bubbly and lightly browned. Serve immediately.

MAKES ABOUT 40 BITES

• •

Secrets: These freeze well. Before baking place cheese bites in a
single layer on a cookie sheet and freeze. When hard, remove from cookie sheet and
put into a large plastic zip-top freezer bag. Store in the freezer until needed.

Bacon cooked on folded paper toweling in a
microwave oven is generally crisper than its fried counterpart.

• •

It is so easy to keep these in the freezer for unexpected
company. Through years of doing the Silver Coffee parties, we have
found it helpful to freeze the cheese bites on disposable aluminum trays which
can be sealed in large plastic zip-top freezer bags. This makes both baking
and clean-up much faster and easier. This method will work well for
other hors d'oeuvres suitable for freezing.

Lasagna with
Tomato-Cream Sauce and Mozzarella

It is important to use fresh lasagna when making this dish.

Tomato-Cream Sauce

½ cup extra-virgin olive oil
4 garlic cloves, minced
   Sea salt, to taste

½ teaspoon hot red pepper flakes, or to
   taste
1 (28-ounce) can crushed tomatoes
1 cup heavy cream

Pasta and Assembly

   Butter
   Grated zest of 1 lemon
   Fresh lasagna noodles (purchase at an
   Italian specialty market)

1 recipe Tomato-Cream Sauce
8 ounces fresh whole milk mozzarella,
   thinly sliced

Tomato-Cream Sauce

In a large unheated skillet, combine oil, garlic, salt, and red pepper flakes, stirring to coat with oil. Cook over medium heat about 2 to 3 minutes or just until garlic turns golden but does not brown. Add crushed tomatoes, and stir to blend. Simmer tomato mixture, uncovered, about 15 minutes or until the sauce begins to thicken. Add cream, stir, and heat for 1 minute. Taste for seasoning.

Pasta and Assembly

Preheat oven to 350 degrees.

Butter a 9 x 13-inch baking dish and sprinkle with lemon zest. Precook lasagna according to package directions. Spoon about ½ cup sauce over the bottom of the baking dish. Cover with 4 slices precooked pasta. Continue layering lasagna and sauce in this manner until all of the sauce and pasta have been used, ending with a layer of pasta. Cover top with mozzarella slices.

Place the baking dish in the center of the oven and bake about 20 minutes or until the cheese is melted and the dish is bubbling. Remove from oven and let stand for 10 minutes before cutting.

SERVES 9

● ●

Secrets: This dish tends to release a fair amount of liquid, so serve with a slotted spoon.

For the Special Occasion Reception make recipe 9 times.

● ●

Yummy Cheese Stars

A Silver Sister's wonderful mother makes these every Christmas.
We like her idea of using a cookie press fitted with the star design.

1	(8-ounce) package extra-sharp Cheddar cheese	1½	cups flour
½	cup (1 stick) margarine (do not use butter)	1	teaspoon baking powder
		¼	teaspoon salt
		¼-½	teaspoon cayenne pepper

Preheat oven to 350 degrees.

Lightly grease baking sheets. Grate Cheddar cheese into a large bowl and add margarine. Beat cheese and margarine until well blended using an electric mixer. Add flour, baking powder, salt, and cayenne to cheese mixture. Continue beating until all ingredients are thoroughly combined. Gather mixture together into a roll using your hands and push through a cookie press fitted with the star design disk (or design disk of your choice). Press stars onto prepared baking sheets. Bake for 10 to 12 minutes (be careful they don't burn). Remove from oven and cool on racks. Store in an airtight container between layers of wax paper. These freeze beautifully.

MAKES 60

Butternut Squash and Apple Soup

2 tablespoons unsalted butter	1½ pounds sweet apples (4 large), such as McIntosh
2 tablespoons good olive oil	2 teaspoons kosher salt
4 cups chopped yellow onions (3 large)	½ teaspoon freshly ground black pepper
2 tablespoons mild curry powder	2 cups water
5 pounds butternut squash (2 large)	2 cups good apple juice or cider

Warm butter and olive oil in a large pot over low heat. Add onions and curry powder and cook, uncovered, for 15 to 20 minutes, until the onions are tender. Stir occasionally, scraping the bottom of the pot.

Peel squash, cut in half, and remove the seeds. Cut squash into chunks. Peel, quarter, and core the apples. Cut into chunks. Add squash, apples, salt, pepper, and 2 cups of water to the pot. Bring to a boil, cover, reduce heat to low, and cook for 30 to 40 minutes, until squash and apples are very soft.

Process the soup through a food mill fitted with a large blade, or purée it coarsely in the bowl of a food processor fitted with a steel blade. Pour soup back into the pot. Add apple juice and enough water to make soup the consistency you like (it should be slightly sweet and quite thick). Check salt and pepper and serve hot.

MAKES 3½ QUARTS

Chicken Gumbo Ya Ya

This is so tasty. It is worth the effort to brown the chicken.

1 large roasting chicken, about 5 pounds, disjointed
Salt
Cayenne pepper
Garlic powder
2½ cups flour, divided
1 cup vegetable oil
2 cups coarsely chopped onions
1½ cups coarsely chopped celery
2 cups coarsely chopped green bell pepper
6 cups chicken stock
1½ teaspoons minced fresh garlic
1 pound andouille sausage, finely chopped (spicy smoked sausage such as kielbasa may be substituted)
4 cups fluffy cooked rice

Cut chicken breasts in half crosswise. This will give you 10 pieces of chicken. Season with salt, cayenne, and garlic and let stand at room temperature for 30 minutes. Put 1½ cups flour in a large paper bag. Add chicken pieces and shake until well coated. Remove chicken pieces and reserve flour.

In a large skillet brown the chicken in very hot oil, remove and set aside. Stir oil remaining in the skillet with a wire whisk to loosen all the brown particles from the bottom and sides of the pan. Whisk in 1 cup of the reserved flour and stir constantly until the mixture of oil and flour (the roux) becomes dark brown. Remove from heat and add onions, celery, and green bell pepper, stirring constantly so they do not burn.

Transfer roux and vegetables to a large heavy saucepan. Add stock to roux and vegetables and bring to a boil, stirring. Lower heat to a quick simmer and add garlic, sausage, and chicken. Continue cooking until chicken is tender, 1¾ to 2 hours. Adjust seasonings and serve in bowls over rice.

SERVES 8

● ●

Secret: For the New Orleans Brunch make this recipe 3 times.

● ●

Snow Pea Soup

*For a ladies' luncheon serve the soup warm or at room temperature
in flowerpot shaped clear votives. They will fit nicely on a luncheon plate with
other items being served, and may be sipped so no soup spoon is necessary.*

4 tablespoons unsalted butter	1 pound snow peas, strings removed
1 small garlic clove, minced	1 cup milk
1 medium red onion, chopped	1 tablespoon grated fresh gingerroot
⅓ cup all-purpose flour	Salt, to taste
3 cups chicken stock	White pepper, to taste

In a large saucepan melt butter over medium heat. Add garlic and onion and cook until soft and translucent, about 5 minutes. Remove from heat, add flour and mix thoroughly. Return to medium heat and cook for three minutes, stirring to make a roux.

Add chicken stock, bring to a boil, reduce heat and simmer, stirring for 2 to 3 minutes or until thickened. Add snow peas and cook for 5 minutes, or until peas are puffed and bright green but not too soft. Pour in milk and cook for 3 minutes longer.

Purée snow pea mixture in a blender or food processor until very smooth. Strain through a fine sieve into the saucepan. Reheat for about 5 minutes. Stir in gingerroot, salt, and pepper to taste. Serve hot.

SERVES 6

● ●

Secret: For the Special Occasion Reception make enough soup for 150 servings.

● ●

Garlic Bread

1 loaf French bread, about 14 inches long	¼ cup finely chopped fresh dill
8 tablespoons (1 stick) unsalted butter	¼ cup freshly grated Parmesan cheese
2 cloves garlic, mashed to a purée	

Preheat oven to 375 degrees.

Slice bread lengthwise. Melt butter in a small skillet, add garlic, and heat gently for 2 minutes. Brush the melted butter generously on the cut sides of the bread. Sprinkle with dill and Parmesan cheese.

Bake until golden and very hot, 5 to 8 minutes. Cut each half crosswise into 1-inch slices and serve immediately.

SERVES 10

● ●

Secret: For the New Orleans Brunch make 3 loaves.

● ●

Pumpkin Muffins with Crystallized Ginger

1   can (15-ounces) unsweetened pumpkin
    purée
2   cups packed brown sugar
1   cup unsalted butter, melted
4   large eggs
½   cup apple cider
3½ cups unbleached all-purpose flour
2   teaspoons baking soda

2   teaspoons baking powder
1   teaspoon salt
4½ teaspoons ground cinnamon
4½ teaspoons ground ginger
1   teaspoon grated nutmeg
½   teaspoon ground cloves
1   cup finely chopped crystallized ginger

Preheat oven to 350 degrees.

Place paper liners in 28 muffin cups. Stir pumpkin, sugar, and butter together in a large mixing bowl. Add eggs and beat until the mixture is smooth. Stir in apple cider. Sift flour, baking soda, baking powder, salt, cinnamon, ground ginger, nutmeg, and cloves into another bowl. Gradually stir flour mixture into the pumpkin mixture until thoroughly mixed. Mix in crystallized ginger until evenly distributed.

Spoon batter into muffin cups, filling each cup almost to the top. Bake 20 to 25 minutes or until puffed and golden. Serve warm with butter.

MAKES 28 MUFFINS

Rich Moist Cornbread

1   cup sour cream
1   (16-ounce) can cream-style corn
2   eggs, lightly beaten
½   cup vegetable oil

1   cup self-rising cornmeal
2   teaspoons baking powder
¼   cup sugar

Preheat oven to 400 degrees.

Grease a 9 x 13-inch baking pan. Mix together sour cream, corn, eggs, and oil until well blended. Mix cornmeal, baking powder, and sugar together and add to moist mixture.

Pour into baking pan. Bake for 30 minutes or until lightly browned.

SERVES 8 TO 12

Asian Spinach Salad

Sesame Dressing

3   tablespoons sesame oil
3   tablespoons salad oil
3   tablespoons white wine vinegar
1½ tablespoons soy sauce

1½ tablespoons dry sherry
1½ tablespoons sugar
¼   teaspoon ground ginger

Salad and Asian Noodles

2   tablespoons vegetable oil
1   (3-ounce) package Asian noodle soup
     mix, noodles coarsely broken
½   cup slivered almonds
2   tablespoons sesame seeds

1   (10-ounce) package spinach or mixed
     Asian greens (found at health food
     stores)
1   bunch green onions, chopped

Sesame Dressing

Place sesame oil, salad oil, vinegar, soy sauce, sherry, sugar, and ginger in a jar and shake until well mixed. Set aside or refrigerate until ready to use.

Asian Noodles

Heat 2 tablespoons oil in heavy medium skillet. Add noodles from soup mix (reserve seasoning packet), almonds, and sesame seeds. Stir until noodles, nuts and seeds are toasted and golden, about 8 minutes. Pour contents of skillet into a large bowl and cool for 10 minutes.

Assembly

Add spinach and green onions to bowl with Asian noodles. Toss with enough dressing to coat.

SERVES 4 TO 6

● ●

Secrets: To prepare ahead for a party, place spinach, onions,
toasted noodles, almonds, sesame seeds into separate containers or zip-top plastic bags.
Just before serving, toss all ingredients together with enough dressing to coat.

For the Pacific Rim Dinner triple this recipe.

● ●

Autumn Turkey Salad

Salad

12 cups chopped turkey breast	4 tablespoons dry white wine
2 cups sliced celery	1½ teaspoons salt
1 (8-ounce) can pineapple tidbits, drained	1½ teaspoons curry powder
2 cups reduced fat mayonnaise or salad dressing	

Fruit for Garnish

2 red delicious apples, thinly sliced	1 pound strawberries, stems removed
1 cantaloupe, thinly sliced	Lettuce leaves
½ pound green grapes, cut into small bunches	¼ cup chopped walnuts, toasted

Salad

Combine turkey, celery and pineapple in a large bowl. Set aside. Combine mayonnaise, wine, salt, and curry powder. Add to chicken mixture, tossing to coat. Cover and refrigerate 1 to 2 hours.

Assembly and Fruit Garnish

Line platter with lettuce leaves. Mound turkey salad in center and garnish with fruit around the rim. Sprinkle toasted walnuts on top of salad.

SERVES 16

● ●

Secret: This salad is best made ahead to let the flavors combine.

● ●

Beet and Orange Salad with Citrus Vinaigrette

Beets and Oranges

3   pounds fresh beets or 3 (15-ounce) cans   2   large navel oranges
      baby beets, drained

Citrus Vinaigrette

6   tablespoons fresh orange juice   1½ teaspoons kosher salt
3   tablespoons fresh lime juice   ½   teaspoon pepper
1   shallot, chopped   7   tablespoons olive oil
½   teaspoon sugar

Beets and Oranges

If using fresh beets, trim off the green tops and place beets in a large pot of salted water to cover. Bring to a boil and simmer uncovered for 50 minutes to 1 hour or until beets are tender. Drain and cool until able to handle.

Peel and chop beets into ½-inch cubes. (If using canned beets, drain the liquid and dice beets into ½-inch cubes.) Using a vegetable peeler, remove zest from oranges (leave the bitter white pith). Cut zest into very thin 1-inch-long pieces. Peel the remaining skin from oranges and divide into sections. Combine beets, orange sections, and orange zest in a medium bowl.

Citrus Vinaigrette

Whisk orange juice, lime juice, shallots, sugar, salt, and pepper in a small bowl. Gradually whisk in olive oil.

Pour dressing over beets and oranges. Cover and refrigerate overnight. It is best to let the mixture marinate a day. Serve cold or at room temperature.

SERVES 8

• •

Secret: For the Special Occasion Reception make recipe 8 times.

• •

Boston Lettuce, Hearts of Palm, and Walnut Salad

Dressing

1 cup walnut oil
9 tablespoons red wine vinegar
1 tablespoon plus 2 teaspoons Dijon
   mustard

1 tablespoon sugar
   Salt and freshly ground black pepper

Salad

4-5 heads butter or Boston lettuce
   (about 1½ to 2 pounds)
2 (14-ounce) cans hearts of palm, drained
   and sliced

¾ cup sliced green onions (1 large bunch)
1 cup (4-ounces) chopped walnuts,
   toasted

Dressing

Pour oil, vinegar, mustard, and sugar into a covered jar. Shake until well blended. Season to taste with salt and pepper. Refrigerate until needed.

Salad

Wash lettuce, dry well, and tear into bite-size pieces. Store in plastic bags and refrigerate until ready to use.

Assembly

When ready to serve, place lettuce, hearts of palm, and green onions in a large bowl. Toss with as much dressing as needed to lightly cover. Add walnuts and gently toss.

SERVES 12

"California Roll" Salad

Sushi Rice Salad with Avocado, Cucumber, and Green Onions

Salad

1½ cups long-grain rice
¼ cup and 3 tablespoons rice vinegar
¼ cup sugar
1½ teaspoons salt
1 tablespoon sesame seeds
(preferably unhulled)
3 tablespoons vegetable oil

2 tablespoons drained, finely chopped
pickled ginger (reserve juice)
4 green onions, cut lengthwise into thin
1-inch strips (about ¾ cup)
½ cup finely shredded carrot
1 large seedless cucumber (about 1 pound),
quartered lengthwise, cored, and
chopped
1 avocado

Dressing

2 teaspoons prepared wasabi
(Japanese green horseradish)
1 tablespoon hot water

2 tablespoons cold water
2 tablespoons soy sauce
2 teaspoons ginger juice (use reserved juice)

Salad

Bring a large pot of salted water to a boil. Stir in rice and boil 10 minutes. Drain rice in a colander and rinse. Set colander over a kettle of boiling water (rice should not touch water) and steam rice, covered with a kitchen towel and lid, until fluffy and dry, 10 to 15 minutes (check water level in kettle occasionally, adding water if necessary).

While rice is steaming, place vinegar, sugar, and salt in a small saucepan and bring to a boil. Stir until sugar is dissolved and remove from heat.

In a dry small skillet toast sesame seeds over moderate heat, stirring, until golden and fragrant. Transfer to a small bowl and set aside.

Put rice in a large bowl and stir in vinegar mixture. Cool rice and stir in sesame seeds, the remaining 3 tablespoons vinegar, oil, ginger, green onions, carrots, and cucumber. Salad may be prepared up to this point 1 day ahead. Cover and refrigerate.

When ready to proceed, bring salad to room temperature. Peel and pit avocado. Quarter avocado and cut crosswise into thin slices. Add avocado to salad and toss well.

Dressing

In a small bowl stir prepared wasabi into hot water and stir in cold water, soy sauce, and ginger juice. Drizzle salad with dressing and serve immediately.

SERVES 6

• •

Secrets: For the Pacific Rim Dinner double this recipe.

To make this easier, find an Asian market for the unusual ingredients.

• •

Citrus Marinated Hearts of Palm Salad

Marinade

½ cup fresh orange juice
¼ cup fresh lime juice
2   tablespoons olive oil
1½ tablespoons honey
1   tablespoon balsamic vinegar
1½ teaspoons Dijon mustard

1½ teaspoons pink peppercorns, lightly
    crushed with side of a knife
1   teaspoon finely chopped fresh tarragon
    Salt and pepper, to taste
1   (14-ounce) can hearts of palm, drained
    and sliced

Salad

4-5 cups mixed baby salad greens

1   tablespoon finely chopped fresh chives

Marinade

Combine orange juice, lime juice, oil, honey, vinegar, mustard, peppercorns, and tarragon in a small bowl and whisk until smooth. Add salt and pepper to taste. Add the hearts of palm and marinate for 1 hour.

Assembly

Drain hearts of palm, reserving marinade. Toss the salad greens with 3 to 4 tablespoons marinade and arrange on salad plates. Arrange hearts of palm on top of greens. Spoon a little more marinade over the palm hearts and sprinkle with chives.

SERVES 4 TO 6

● ●

Secret: For the Special Occasion Reception make recipe 12 times.

● ●

Grape Tomato Salad

4 pints grape tomatoes
   Good quality olive oil
   Balsamic vinegar

Kosher salt or Jane's Krazy Mixed-Up
   Salt
Freshly ground black pepper

Cut grape tomatoes in half. Place in serving bowl. Drizzle with olive oil and vinegar. Add salt and pepper to taste.

SERVES 16

Green Salad with Creole Green Onion Dressing

Leave it to New Orleans for salad with a punch!

Salad Dressing

1 egg	1 tablespoon Creole seasoning
1 egg yolk	Dash of hot pepper sauce
1 cup salad oil, divided	3 tablespoons chopped green onions
2 tablespoons lemon juice	½ tablespoon Creole or Dijon mustard
¼ teaspoon salt	

Salad

7 (10-ounce) bags mixed salad greens

Dressing

Place egg, egg yolk, and ¼ cup salad oil in a blender container with salt, Creole seasoning, and hot pepper sauce. Cover and blend at low speed. Remove cover and gradually add remaining salad oil and lemon juice in a steady stream (mixture will be thick and creamy). Add mustard and green onions and blend at high speed until thoroughly combined. Place dressing in an airtight container and refrigerate until needed.

MAKES 1½ CUPS

Assembly

Prepare salad greens by washing and drying thoroughly. Toss salad greens with dressing. Be light-handed with the dressing, adding it in as you toss the greens.

SERVES 24

The best way to toss a big salad is with your hands – clean, of course! Either toss in bunches, or use a bowl twice the size of the ingredients. On occasion, for very large volumes, we have used a clean ice chest. You need room to toss properly.

Marinated Asparagus and Hearts of Palm Salad

1½ pounds fresh asparagus
1 (14-ounce) can hearts of palm, drained and cut into ½-inch slices
½ cup good olive oil
¼ cup cider vinegar
1-2 cloves garlic, crushed
¾ teaspoon salt
½ teaspoon pepper
Cherry or grape tomatoes

Snap off tough ends of asparagus. Remove scales from stalks with a vegetable peeler, if desired. Cook in boiling water to cover for 3 minutes or until crisp-tender, drain. Plunge asparagus into ice water to stop the cooking process, drain well and pat dry.

Combine asparagus and hearts of palm in a zip-top, heavy-duty plastic bag. Combine oil, vinegar, garlic, salt, and pepper. Shake until well mixed. Pour dressing over vegetables. Seal bag and marinate in refrigerator overnight.

When ready to serve, arrange asparagus on lettuce lined platter or individual salad plates and garnish with tomatoes.

SERVES 8

Maw-Maw's Slaw

½ pound (about 2 cups) shredded white cabbage
½ pound (about 2 cups) shredded red cabbage
½ pound (8-ounces) shredded assorted greens, such as mustard greens, collards, or spinach, trimmed and washed (about 2 cups)
1 cup thinly sliced red onions
1 cup chopped green onions, green parts only
½ cup chopped parsley
1¼ cups mayonnaise
¼ cup Creole or whole grain mustard
1 teaspoon salt
¼ teaspoon freshly ground black pepper
¼ teaspoon cayenne pepper
1 teaspoon sugar

Place white cabbage, red cabbage, greens, red onions, green onions and parsley in a large salad bowl.

In a small bowl, combine mayonnaise, mustard, salt, black pepper, cayenne, and sugar. Mix well. Add the mixture to the greens and toss to mix thoroughly.

Cover and refrigerate for at least 1 hour. Serve chilled.

SERVES 10 TO 12

Romaine Salad with Prosciutto Crisps

The small inner leaves of Romaine lettuce are tender and crisp, perfect for this salad.

Prosciutto Crisps
Olive oil

8 slices prosciutto (about 4-ounces)

Salad Dressing
1 teaspoon grated lemon zest
3 tablespoons fresh lemon juice
2 garlic cloves, minced
1 teaspoon white wine vinegar

⅔ cup extra virgin olive oil
1 teaspoon ground black pepper
½ teaspoon salt

Salad
2 (10-ounce) bags hearts of romaine, torn into pieces

2 ounces Pecorino Romano cheese, shaved

Prosciutto Crisps
Preheat oven to 400 degrees.

Lightly brush a baking sheet with olive oil, and arrange prosciutto in a single layer. Bake about 5 to 10 minutes or until crisp. Remove from oven and cool on a wire rack.

Salad Dressing
Combine lemon zest, juice, garlic, and vinegar in a small bowl, and whisk well. Slowly add olive oil, whisking constantly until smooth. Add pepper and salt. Set aside.

MAKES 1 CUP

Assembly
Place romaine in a large salad bowl. Add salad dressing and shaved Pecorino Romano, and toss to combine. Serve topped with prosciutto crisps.

SERVES 8

● ●

Secret: Use a vegetable peeler to shave the Pecorino Romano cheese.

For the Special Occasion Reception make recipe 12 times.

● ●

Spinach Salad with Pine Nuts, Apples and Bacon

Dressing

½ cup olive oil
2 tablespoons white wine vinegar
2 teaspoons Dijon mustard
1 teaspoon soy sauce

½ teaspoon curry powder
¼ teaspoon sugar
    Salt and freshly ground pepper

Salad

4-5 (5-ounce) bags pre-washed baby organic spinach
1 large green apple, coarsely chopped

6 pieces bacon, cooked very crisp and crumbled
¼ cup pine nuts, toasted to a light brown

Dressing

Put oil, vinegar, mustard, soy sauce, curry, sugar, salt, and pepper in a covered jar and shake until well blended. Refrigerate until ready to use.

Assembly

Pour dressing in bottom of salad bowl. Place spinach in bowl on top of dressing, then apples and bacon on top of that, but do not toss. Cover and refrigerate. When ready to serve, toss salad and sprinkle with toasted pine nuts.

SERVES 8

Roasted Grape Tomatoes with Basil

2 pints grape tomatoes
    Good olive oil
    Kosher salt

    Freshly ground black pepper
10 fresh basil leaves, slivered

Preheat oven to 400 degrees.

Place tomatoes on a baking sheet and drizzle with olive oil. Spread tomatoes into one layer and sprinkle liberally with salt and pepper. Roast for 15 to 20 minutes or until the tomatoes are soft. Transfer to a serving platter and top with basil leaves. Serve hot or at room temperature.

SERVES 8

• •

Secrets: For the Holiday Cocktail Buffet make this recipe 9 times.

To sliver basil leaves, it is easiest to roll several leaves lengthwise and cut crosswise into tiny strips.

• •

Summer Salad with Strawberries, Mandarin Oranges, and Toasted Almonds

Dressing

⅔ cup olive oil
⅓ cup orange juice
¼ cup sugar
3 tablespoons vinegar

1 teaspoon celery seed
   Salt and pepper to taste
   Dash of dry mustard

Salad

3 (10-ounce) bags mixed greens
1 (11-ounce) can Mandarin orange
   sections, well-drained
4 cups sliced fresh strawberries

1 cup chopped green onions
1 (4-ounce) container feta cheese
⅓ cup sliced almonds, toasted

Dressing

Combine oil, orange juice, sugar, vinegar, celery seed, salt, pepper, and dry mustard in a covered jar and shake well. Refrigerate until ready to use.

Assembly

Wash and dry lettuce, and combine with orange sections, strawberries, onions, feta cheese, and almonds. Add the salad dressing and toss until well coated.

SERVES 10

For variety, try changing the fruits, type of cheese and nuts used, like grapefruit sections or sliced apples instead of strawberries; blue cheese instead of feta; toasted pecans, walnuts or pine nuts instead of almonds – the combinations are infinite. Try adding dried cherries or cranberries for a Fall flavor.

Green Beans with Caramelized Onions and Blue Cheese

1½ pounds green beans, stem ends
  trimmed
⅓ cup plus 2 tablespoons olive oil
3 tablespoons plus 2 teaspoons sherry or
  balsamic vinegar
2 tablespoons chopped fresh thyme or
  2 teaspoons dried

2 teaspoons soy sauce
1 teaspoon sugar
  Salt
  Freshly ground black pepper
3 large red onions, sliced
1 cup crumbled blue cheese

Cook green beans in boiling water until crisp-tender. Drain and immediately plunge in ice water to stop cooking and set color. Drain again.

To make vinaigrette, combine ⅓ cup oil, vinegar, thyme, soy sauce, sugar, salt, and pepper in a covered jar and shake well.

Preheat oven to 350 degrees.

Arrange onion slices on a baking sheet, brush with remaining oil and some of the vinaigrette. Roast, turning once, 8 to 12 minutes or until deep brown.

To serve place beans in a large bowl. Add the remaining dressing and toss to coat. Arrange the beans on a platter and top with onions. Drizzle with dressing remaining in bowl. Sprinkle evenly with blue cheese. Serve at room temperature.

SERVES 8 TO 10

● ●

Secret: For the Holiday Cocktail Buffet make this recipe 8 times.

● ●

Oven-Roasted New Potatoes

3 pounds small red-skinned new potatoes
  (about 20)
½ cup good olive oil

1½ teaspoons kosher salt
1 teaspoon freshly ground black pepper
2 tablespoons minced garlic (6 cloves)

Preheat oven to 400 degrees.

Cut the potatoes in half or quarters and place in a bowl with the olive oil, salt, pepper, and garlic. Toss until the potatoes are well coated. Spread the potatoes in a single layer on a heavy baking sheet. Bake until the potatoes are crisp and browned, about 45 minutes. Season to taste and serve.

SERVES 10

Potato-Fennel Gratin

2 small (4 cups) sliced fennel bulbs	2 cups plus 2 tablespoons heavy cream
1 yellow onion, thinly sliced	2½ cups (½ pound) Gruyère cheese
2 tablespoons good olive oil	1 teaspoon kosher salt
1 tablespoon unsalted butter	½ teaspoon freshly ground black pepper
2 pounds (4 large) russet potatoes	

Preheat oven to 350 degrees.

Butter a 10 x 15 x 2-inch baking dish. Remove stalks from fennel and cut bulbs in half lengthwise. Remove cores and thinly slice bulbs crosswise.

In a large skillet, mix olive oil and butter together over medium-low heat, add fennel and onion, cook for about 15 minutes or until tender.

Peel potatoes, and thinly slice. Mix sliced potatoes in a large bowl with 2 cups cream, 2 cups Gruyère, salt, and pepper. Add cooked fennel and onion and mix well.

Pour potato mixture into the baking dish. Press down to even and smooth out the potatoes. Mix together the remaining 2 tablespoons of cream and ½ cup of Gruyère and sprinkle on the top. Bake for 1½ hours or until the potatoes are very tender and the top is browned and bubbly. Allow to sit for 10 minutes before serving.

SERVES 8

Spinach Gratin

4 tablespoons (½ stick) unsalted butter	5 (10-ounce) packages chopped spinach, thawed
4 cups chopped yellow onions	1 cup freshly grated Parmesan cheese, divided
¼ cup all-purpose flour	1 tablespoon kosher salt
¼ teaspoon grated nutmeg	½ teaspoon ground black pepper
1 cup heavy cream	½ cup grated Gruyère cheese
2 cups milk	

Preheat oven to 425 degrees.

Melt butter in a heavy pan over medium heat. Add onions, cook and stir until translucent, about 15 minutes. Add flour and nutmeg and cook, stirring, for 2 more minutes. Add cream and milk and cook until thickened.

Squeeze as much liquid as possible from the spinach and add spinach to the sauce. Add ½ cup of Parmesan cheese and mix well. Season to taste with salt and pepper.

Transfer spinach mixture to a baking dish and top with the remaining ½ cup Parmesan and the Gruyère. Bake for 20 minutes, or until hot and bubbly. Serve immediately.

SERVES 8 TO 10

Potato-Turnip Purée

4   large potatoes, peeled and cubed
1   medium yellow turnip, peeled and
    cubed
1   medium onion, peeled and cut into
    chunks
2   tablespoons butter, softened
    Milk

1   (3-ounce) package cream cheese,
    softened
½   cup sour cream
4   teaspoons prepared horseradish
    Salt
    Ground black pepper

Preheat oven to 350 degrees.

Grease a 2-quart baking dish. Place potatoes, turnip, and onion in a large saucepan, cover with salted water and bring to a boil. Reduce heat and simmer about 30 minutes or until fork tender.

When the vegetables are tender, drain and mash them adding butter and enough milk to moisten. Stir in cream cheese, sour cream and horseradish. Season liberally with salt and pepper.

Spoon mixture into the baking dish and bake uncovered for 20 minutes.

SERVES 12

• •

Secrets: For the Holiday Cocktail Buffet menu make this recipe 6 times.

Can be made one day ahead before baking. Cover and refrigerate
until ready to bake. Bring to room temperature before baking.

• •

Provençal Tomatoes

6 ripe tomatoes (2½ to 3-inches in diameter)
1½ cups fresh white bread crumbs
   (5 slices, crusts removed)
2 green onions, minced
¼ cup minced fresh basil leaves
2 tablespoons minced fresh flat-leaf
   parsley

2 cloves garlic, minced
½ teaspoon minced fresh thyme leaves
1 teaspoon salt
   Kosher salt
   Ground black pepper
½ cup grated Gruyère cheese
   High quality olive oil

Preheat oven to 400 degrees.

Core the tomatoes, removing as little flesh as possible. Cut them in half crosswise, remove seeds and juice. Place tomato halves in a baking dish.

In a bowl, combine bread crumbs, green onions, basil, parsley, garlic, thyme, and salt. Sprinkle tomato halves generously with salt and pepper. Using your hands or a spoon, fill cavities and cover tops of tomatoes with bread crumb mixture.

Bake tomatoes for 15 minutes, or until they are tender. Sprinkle with cheese, drizzle with olive oil, and bake for 30 seconds more. May be served hot or at room temperature. Can be made ahead and refrigerated. Bake before serving.

SERVES 8

● ●

Secret: To make fresh bread crumbs, remove the crusts of good, fine-grained white bread. Cut the bread into cubes and pulse in a food processor until finely minced.

● ●

Roasted Brussels Sprouts

This recipe elevates Brussels sprouts to a whole new status. They are
addictive and are equally good the next day straight from the refrigerator.

2   tablespoons olive oil
3   pounds Brussels sprouts, trimmed and
     halved if large
6   ounces thinly sliced pancetta, chopped
2   garlic cloves, finely chopped

    Kosher salt
    Freshly ground black pepper
3   tablespoons balsamic vinegar
1   tablespoon chopped fresh thyme

Preheat oven to 450 degrees.

Spray a heavy rimmed baking sheet with oil. Place 2 tablespoons oil in a large zip-top plastic bag. Place Brussels sprouts, pancetta, and garlic in the bag and shake gently until Brussels sprouts are coated with oil. Add salt and pepper and shake again.

Spread mixture in a single layer on prepared baking sheet. Roast until Brussels sprouts are brown and crispy, stirring often, about 20 minutes. (Can be made 3 hours ahead. Let stand at room temperature.) Before serving, drizzle Brussels sprouts with vinegar and sprinkle with thyme. Stir to coat. Return to 450 degree oven and roast until heated through, about 5 minutes.

SERVES 8

● ●

Secret: Pancetta, Italian bacon cured in salt, is available at
Italian markets or in the refrigerated deli case of many grocery stores.

● ●

Garlic Cheese Grits

4 cups water	¾ pound processed cheese loaf (Velveeta), cubed
1 teaspoon salt	
2-3 garlic cloves, minced	2 eggs, slightly beaten
1 cup grits	¾ cup milk
½ cup (1 stick) butter	1 cup grated sharp Cheddar cheese

Preheat oven to 350 degrees.

Place 4 cups water in a large pot, add salt and garlic and bring to a boil. Add grits, reduce heat, and cook until slightly thickened, stirring frequently. Remove from heat. Add butter and processed cheese, stirring until melted. Beat eggs and add enough milk to make 1 cup. Stir egg mixture slowly into grits.

Pour into a greased 3-quart baking dish and bake for 45 minutes. Sprinkle grated Cheddar cheese on top and return to oven to brown.

SERVES 12

• •

Secret: The casserole may seem like jello in the middle but firms up nicely upon cooling. This dish can be made ahead and baked later.

• •

Curried Couscous

This couscous has the most delicious blend of flavors and is so easy to make.

1½ cups couscous
1   tablespoon unsalted butter
1½ cups boiling water
¼   cup plain yogurt
¼   cup good olive oil
1   teaspoon white wine vinegar
1   teaspoon curry powder
¼   teaspoon ground turmeric
1½ teaspoons kosher salt

1   teaspoon black pepper, freshly ground
½   cup grated carrots
½   cup minced flat leaf parsley
½   cup dried currants
¼   cup sliced almonds
2   green onions, thinly sliced (white and green parts)
¼   small red onion, finely chopped

Place couscous in a medium bowl. Melt butter in boiling water and pour over couscous. Cover tightly and allow the couscous to soak for 5 minutes. Fluff with a fork.

Whisk together yogurt, olive oil, vinegar, curry, turmeric, salt, and pepper. Pour over the fluffed couscous and mix well with a fork. Add the carrots, parsley, currants, almonds, scallions, and red onions and mix well. If needed, adjust seasonings. Serve at room temperature.

SERVES 10

This also makes a great base for a salad, if you have leftovers. Just add cooked chicken or turkey cubes, or cooked shrimp in summer – or cooked lamb, pork or beef in winter.

Nutty Browned Brown Rice

No, you aren't seeing double, but you will want seconds.

¾ cup (1½ sticks) unsalted butter, divided
3 large shallots, peeled and quartered
1 heaping handful of pearl onions, cleaned and peeled
1 cup brown rice
1 can French onion soup

2 cans chicken broth
1-2 cups white wine
1 (8-ounce) can sliced mushrooms or 1 (8-ounce) box fresh mushrooms, cooked in 1 tablespoon butter
1 cup toasted pecans, chopped

Melt ½ stick butter in a saucepan over medium heat, add shallots and pearl onions, and cook until soft. Set aside.

Melt the remaining 1 stick butter in another saucepan over medium-high heat, add brown rice, and cook until rice is browned and nut-colored, stirring constantly.

Combine soup, broth, 1 cup wine, mushrooms, pecans, and reserved onion mixture with browned rice. Immediately reduce heat to low and cover. Simmer 20 to 30 minutes, checking occasionally to make sure rice does not get too dry, adding more wine if needed. Cook until rice is al dente (tender to the tooth). The rice is done when all liquid is absorbed (presuming enough liquid is added during the cooking process and remembering that all rice is different).

SERVES 8

● ●

Secret: Pearl onions come in multiple colors, and the dish is made more interesting by using a variety. Chopped portobella mushrooms add extra pizzazz.

● ●

Zucchini Creole

3   medium zucchini, unpeeled
3   tablespoons butter
3   tablespoons flour
1   (28-ounce) can chopped tomatoes, slightly drained
1   small green pepper, chopped

1   small onion, chopped
1   teaspoon salt
1   tablespoon brown sugar
1   bay leaf
1   cup (4-ounces) grated Cheddar cheese

Preheat oven to 350 degrees.

Slice zucchini into ¼-inch rounds. Place zucchini in a 2-quart baking dish. Set aside.

Melt butter in a medium saucepan over medium heat. Stir in flour until well combined. The mixture will be thick. Add tomatoes, green pepper, onion, salt, brown sugar, and bay leaf. Cook ingredients for 5 minutes or until thick. Pour over zucchini. Sprinkle grated cheese over top. Bake for 1 hour. Serve immediately.

SERVES 8

● ●

Secret: You can assemble this dish a day ahead, then bake it before serving.

● ●

Sweets

Any event, fancy or plain, deserves to
have a sweet ending.

Bananas Foster Bread Pudding

The classic flavors of rum and brown sugar, reminiscent
of the original Bananas Foster, create this delicious bread pudding.

Bread Pudding

3 eggs	1 tablespoon banana extract
½ cup whipping cream	4 cups milk
1 cup granulated sugar	¼ cup butter
1 cup (packed) brown sugar	1 loaf (16-ounce) stale French bread, cut
¼ cup rum	into 1-inch cubes

Sauce

1½ cups (3 sticks) butter	1½ teaspoons banana extract
1½ cups (packed) brown sugar	6 bananas, sliced
¾ cup rum	

Bread Pudding

Preheat oven to 325 degrees.

Stir together eggs, cream, granulated sugar, brown sugar, rum, and banana extract in a large bowl. Heat milk and butter in a large saucepan over medium-high heat until melted, stirring constantly. Do not boil. Stir about one-fourth of hot milk mixture gradually into egg mixture. Add this to the remaining hot milk mixture, stirring constantly.

Place bread cubes in a lightly greased 9 x 13-inch baking dish. Pour egg mixture evenly over bread cubes. Press down on bread to absorb mixture. Bake for 45 to 55 minutes. Remove from oven, and let stand 30 minutes before serving.

Sauce

Combine butter, brown sugar, rum, banana extract, and bananas in a saucepan over medium-high heat and cook, stirring constantly. Do not boil. Remove from heat.

To serve, scoop bread pudding into bowls and top with sauce.

SERVES 10 TO 12

• •

Secret: For the New Orleans Brunch double recipe.

The sauce is also delicious over vanilla ice cream.

• •

Maple Mousse in Chocolate Cups

1 envelope unflavored gelatin
⅓ cup cold water
3 large eggs, separated
⅓ cup light brown sugar
1 cup dark amber maple syrup
2 tablespoons dark rum

¼ cup granulated sugar
2 cups whipping cream
3 boxes (18 per box) purchased cordial-size chocolate cups
Chocolate shavings, for garnish (use a vegetable peeler to shave)

Sprinkle gelatin over cold water and set aside to soften for 5 minutes. Place egg yolks, brown sugar, and maple syrup in the top of a double boiler and stir to combine. Cook over simmering water, stirring constantly, until slightly thickened, 7 to 8 minutes.

Remove from heat, add gelatin, and stir to dissolve. Cool completely, then refrigerate until the mixture begins to set, 15 to 20 minutes.

Stir in rum. Beat egg whites until soft peaks form. Beat in granulated sugar, 1 tablespoon at a time, and continue to beat until stiff and shiny. Gently fold half the egg whites into the maple mixture to lighten, then fold in remaining whites. Beat cream until soft peaks form. Fold whipped cream into the maple mixture.

Place mousse in an airtight container and refrigerate overnight.

Pipe or spoon mousse into prepared chocolate cups. Refrigerate until ready to serve. Sprinkle with chocolate shavings before serving.

MAKES 54

• •

Secrets: Find cordial-size chocolate serving cups at a specialty food store.

This recipe for Maple Mousse makes a lot. Reserve it for another use or buy more chocolate cups.

• •

Raisin Bread Pudding with Vanilla Sauce

Raisin Bread

1 (1-pound) loaf of good quality
   cinnamon raisin bread
½ cup (1 stick) unsalted butter, melted
6 eggs
4 cups milk

1 cup granulated sugar
½ cup raisins
1 tablespoon vanilla
1½ teaspoons cinnamon

Vanilla Sauce

1 cup heavy cream
¼ cup sugar
2 egg yolks
1½ teaspoons all-purpose flour

1½ teaspoons vanilla
⅛ teaspoon salt
1 medium scoop vanilla ice cream

Raisin Bread

Preheat oven to 375 degrees.

Cut bread into 1-inch squares, spread on a baking sheet, and toast in oven until light brown, about 8 minutes. Pack the toasted bread into a 2½-quart baking dish, or 8 (1-cup) ramekins and drizzle with melted butter.

In a medium bowl, whisk together eggs, milk, and sugar until sugar is dissolved. Add the raisins, vanilla, and cinnamon. Pour the custard over the bread and let soak about 10 minutes.

Reduce oven temperature to 350 degrees. Bake the pudding until slightly puffed and firm, about 45 minutes. Cool slightly and serve warm with Vanilla Sauce.

Vanilla Sauce

In a small saucepan, combine cream and sugar and bring to a boil, stirring to dissolve sugar. In a small bowl, whisk together egg yolks, flour, vanilla, and salt until smooth and pale yellow. Pour a little of the hot cream into the yolk mixture, whisking rapidly until smooth, then pour yolk mixture back into pan of cream.

Cook over very low heat (do not boil), stirring constantly with a wooden spoon, until cream has thickened slightly. (To test, run finger across the back of the cream-coated spoon. If it leaves a trace, the sauce is ready.) Remove from heat, stir in the scoop of ice cream until melted. Finally, strain the sauce through a fine sieve. Serve warm or at room temperature over the warm Raisin Bread

SERVES 8

Chocolate Mousse Meringue Kisses

These delicious morsels were devoured at one Silver Sister's book club meeting.

Meringue

5   egg whites
    Pinch cream of tartar
¾ cup sugar

1¾ cups powdered sugar
⅓ cup unsweetened cocoa

Mousse

13 (1-ounce squares) semisweet chocolate
7   egg whites
¼ teaspoon cream of tartar
3   cups heavy cream

1½ teaspoons vanilla
    Chocolate covered coffee beans, for
    garnish

Meringue

Preheat oven to 300 degrees.

In a large bowl beat egg whites with a pinch of cream of tartar until they hold soft peaks. Beat in sugar, 2 tablespoons at a time. Continue beating until the meringue holds very stiff peaks. Sift together powdered sugar and cocoa. Gently fold this mixture into the meringue.

Cover baking sheets with parchment paper. Make bite size meringues by using a small spoon to place 1-inch dollops of meringue on the parchment paper. Lightly moisten a finger with water and pat the meringues into a bird nest shape, increasing the diameter to about 1½-inches.

Bake for 1¼ hours, alternating baking sheets for even baking. When done, transfer meringues to racks and let them cool.

Mousse

While meringues are baking, make the mousse. Melt the chocolate in a double boiler set over hot water. (You may also microwave on high for about 3 minutes, stir to blend.) Let chocolate cool.

In a large bowl, beat 7 egg whites with ¼ teaspoon cream of tartar until they hold stiff peaks. In another bowl, whip well-chilled cream with 1½ teaspoons vanilla until the cream holds stiff peaks. Fold the cooled chocolate carefully into the egg whites. Finally, fold in the whipped cream.

Assembly

Place chocolate mousse in a zip-top plastic bag. Cut ½-inch off one corner. Pipe a generous dollop of mousse onto each meringue and garnish with a chocolate covered coffee bean.

MAKES 100

• •

Secret: To make the meringue dollops uniform, we like to use a 1-inch ice cream scoop.

• •

The Chocolate Mousse Meringue Kisses can be made as a cake. Cover baking sheets with parchment paper and trace three 8-inch squares using an inverted 8-inch square cake pan as a guide. Divide the meringue among the squares, spreading it evenly to the edges. Bake as directed in master recipe. To assemble, place one cooled meringue on a cake stand or plate. Spread chocolate mousse thickly over meringue. Top with a second meringue and spread it thickly with mousse. Place the remaining meringue layer over mousse. Place the leftover mousse in a pastry bag fitted with a decorative tip. Decorate the top of the cake with rows of overlapping figure eights. Lightly cover the cake and refrigerate for 4 hours or overnight. This cake may be kept for up to 48 hours.

SERVES 8

Old-Fashioned Apple Crisp

This won rave reviews at our tasting. It is so good it doesn't need ice cream.

8   Golden Delicious apples (about 4 pounds), peeled, cored, and cut into ⅓-inch-thick slices
3   tablespoons plus 1 cup sugar
1   cup old-fashioned oats
1   cup all-purpose flour
2   teaspoons ground cinnamon
¾   cup (1½ sticks) unsalted butter
     Vanilla ice cream

Preheat oven to 350 degrees.

Butter a 13 x 9 x 2-inch glass baking dish. Combine apples and 3 tablespoons sugar in a large bowl and toss to coat. Transfer to prepared dish.

Combine oats, flour, cinnamon and remaining 1 cup sugar in medium bowl. Add butter with a pastry cutter or 2 knives until pea-size clumps form. Sprinkle over apples. Bake until apples are tender, about 1 hour. Serve with ice cream.

SERVES 8

Banana Strudel

Banana Filling

6 ripe bananas, peeled and cut into ½-inch pieces
½ cup raisins
Juice and grated zest of 1 lemon
1 cinnamon stick

2 tablespoons dark rum
3 tablespoons packed brown sugar
1 tablespoon cornstarch
2 tablespoons banana liqueur (optional)

Strudel

8 sheets phyllo dough, thawed
⅓ cup melted butter
¼ cup granulated sugar

¼ cup finely chopped toasted pecans or macadamia nuts
¼ cup powdered sugar

Banana Filling

Combine bananas, raisins, lemon juice, lemon zest, cinnamon stick, rum, and brown sugar in a heavy saucepan. Simmer the mixture, uncovered, over medium heat until the bananas are just tender, 2 to 3 minutes. Remove from heat, correct flavorings, adding sugar or lemon juice to taste.

Make a paste with cornstarch and banana liqueur or water. Return banana mixture to the heat. Whisk paste into mixture and boil over high heat about 20 seconds or until mixture thickens. Transfer filling to a bowl and let it cool to room temperature. Remove cinnamon stick and set aside.

Strudel

Place a dishtowel covered with plastic wrap on a baking sheet. Lay one sheet of phyllo on the plastic wrap with the long edge toward you. Keep unused phyllo dough covered with plastic wrap and a damp dishtowel. Lightly brush phyllo with melted butter. Sprinkle with granulated sugar and pecans. Lay another sheet of phyllo on top, brush with butter, and sprinkle with sugar and pecans. Repeat with a third and fourth sheet of phyllo.

Mound half the Banana Filling along the long edge closest to you and roll up the phyllo halfway, lifting the dishtowel to help with the rolling. Tuck in the ends and continue rolling the strudel. It should look like a giant egg roll. Carefully roll onto a baking sheet. Assemble the second strudel the same way.

Brush tops of the strudels with remaining butter and sprinkle with remaining sugar and nuts. Cover with plastic wrap and refrigerate until firm, about 30 minutes.

Preheat oven to 375 degrees.

Remove strudel from refrigerator. Using a sharp knife, lightly score the tops of the strudels without cutting all the way through to the filling. Bake strudels 30 to 40 minutes or until golden brown. Transfer strudels to a wire rack to cool for at least 5 minutes. Cut strudels diagonally into slices. Sprinkle with powdered sugar.

MAKES ABOUT 32 SLICES

• •

Secret: For the Special Occasion Reception double recipe.

• •

Coconut and Toasted Almond Rum Squares

These easy, delicious rum squares have always been a hit at our parties.
They are a wonderful make-ahead treat and great to have on hand in your freezer.

1 purchased angel food cake (a loaf cake
   is easiest for this purpose)
1 box 10x powdered sugar
1 cup (2 sticks) unsalted butter, melted

½ cup rum
1 large bag coconut flakes
2 (6-ounce) bags slivered almonds, toasted
   and chopped in a food processor

Cut angel food cake into ¾-inch squares. Combine powdered sugar, butter and rum. Mix until smooth and of a somewhat soupy consistency. Dip squares into frosting, and immediately roll into shredded coconut or toasted, chopped almonds. Set aside on wax paper until frosting hardens. These freeze beautifully in airtight containers and can be made weeks ahead.

MAKES APPROXIMATELY 7 TO 8 DOZEN

• •

Secret: These squares can be made larger
(similar to petit fours) and decorated in any way desired.

• •

Make an assembly line when dipping cake squares.
Line up cake squares, frosting, a bowl for shredded coconut and
a bowl for chopped toasted almonds and waxed paper. This makes it
easy to dip and roll cakes, then place on wax paper to harden. When
frosting in dipping bowl starts to harden, simply put bowl in
the microwave and cook for a few seconds, allowing it to warm
up and soften. When preparing to freeze, stack squares
between sheets of wax paper in an airtight container.

Cocos

These are tasty little cookies. They are easy to make and freeze beautifully.

1½ cups all-purpose flour, unsifted
⅛ teaspoon salt
3¼ cups unsweetened coconut, medium
    shred, divided

1 cup and 6 tablespoons (2¾ sticks)
    unsalted butter, room temperature
1 cup granulated sugar
1 egg yolk

In a medium bowl, blend flour, salt and 2½ cups of coconut briefly with a wire whisk. Set mixture aside.

In a large bowl, use an electric mixer and beat butter at medium-low speed until smooth. Add sugar and beat at medium speed until creamy. Add egg yolk, and beat until slightly fluffy, scraping down the sides of the bowl. At lower speed, gradually blend in coconut mixture until thoroughly combined.

Divide the dough into 8 equal portions. Form each portion into a cylinder 9-inches long and 1-inch in diameter. Place ¾ cup remaining coconut in a shallow dish and roll each cylinder back and forth to cover well. Wrap cylinders in plastic wrap and refrigerate until firm, at least 4 hours. Dough may be refrigerated up to one week, or may be frozen, well wrapped, up to a month. Defrost before baking.

To Bake

Preheat oven to 325 degrees and adjust rack to lower third of oven.

Line two large baking sheets with parchment paper. Using a serrated knife, gently cut dough into ¼-inch thick rounds. Place 1-inch apart on baking sheet. Bake, one sheet at a time, for 8 minutes or until lightly golden around the edges. Place baking sheet on a wire rack to cool 5 minutes. Remove cookies from baking sheet with a spatula and place on rack to cool. Stack cookies, between sheets of wax paper, in an airtight container, and store at room temperature up to 1 week or freeze for several months.

12 DOZEN COOKIES

• •

Secret: You can find unsweetened coconut at a health food store.

• •

Cranberry-Nut Rugalach

This is one of the best variations of Rugalach we've tasted. A great make ahead treat.

Pastry

2 cups unbleached all-purpose flour
1 cup (2 sticks) unsalted butter, chilled,
   cut into small pieces

1 large egg yolk
¾ cup sour cream
   Pinch of salt

Cranberry-Nut Filling

¾ cup dried figs, minced
½ cup dried apricots, minced
½ cup golden raisins
2 cups fresh cranberries
1 tablespoon honey

½ cup (packed) light brown sugar
2 tablespoons orange liqueur
   (Grand Marnier)
½ cup walnuts, finely chopped

Topping

3 tablespoons unsalted butter, melted
¼ cup coarse granulated sugar

2 teaspoons ground cinnamon

Pastry

Place all ingredients in a food processor fitted with a steel blade, and process just until dough resembles coarse meal. Do not let dough begin to form a ball or it will not be as flaky as it should be. Instead turn dough out onto a smooth surface and loosely bring it together with your hands. Wrap securely in plastic wrap and refrigerate at least 3 hours or overnight.

Cranberry-Nut Filling

Place figs, apricots, raisins, cranberries, honey, brown sugar, and Grand Marnier in a medium-size saucepan. Cook, stirring frequently, over medium heat until cranberries have popped and released their juices, 10 to 15 minutes. Transfer mixture to a food processor fitted with a steel blade, and process to blend together (it will not get completely smooth). Add walnuts and pulse just to incorporate. Transfer mixture to a bowl and let cool to room temperature.

Assembly

Divide pastry dough equally into 4 pieces. Work with 1 piece at a time and keep the others refrigerated. On a lightly floured surface, roll each piece into an approximate 9-inch circle. Spread one quarter of the filling mixture evenly over the surface of the dough. With a sharp knife or pastry cutter, cut the circle into 12 equal wedges as if you were cutting a pizza. Beginning with the outside edge of each wedge, roll tightly to the center to make a crescent. Place rugalach 1-inch apart pointed end down on an ungreased baking sheet. Repeat the process with the remaining dough and filling, keeping the assembled pastries refrigerated while working.

Topping

Preheat oven to 350 degrees.

Remove rugalach from refrigerator and brush with melted butter. Combine sugar and cinnamon and sprinkle generously over pastries. Place on baking sheet and bake 20 to 25 minutes or until golden brown. Serve slightly warm or at room temperature. Store extras in zip-top plastic bags in freezer and thaw when needed.

MAKES 48

French Breakfast Puffs

We used this recipe at a daytime Silver Coffee in the early eighties. They are just as delicious two decades later. They are reminiscent of a melt-in-your-mouth donut, but baked not fried!

⅓ cup shortening	½ teaspoon salt
1 cup sugar, divided	¼ teaspoon ground nutmeg
1 egg	½ cup milk
1½ cups all-purpose flour	1 teaspoon ground cinnamon
1½ teaspoons baking powder	½ cup (1 stick) melted butter

Preheat oven to 350 degrees.

Lightly grease miniature muffin pans. Beat together ½ cup sugar and shortening in a large bowl using an electric mixer. Beat in the egg until smooth and creamy.

Sift together flour, baking powder, salt, and nutmeg. Add flour mixture to butter mixture alternating with the milk, beating well after each addition.

Fill muffin pans ¾ full and bake for 10 to 15 minutes or until tops of the puffs spring back when lightly touched.

Mix together cinnamon and reserved sugar. Remove puffs from oven and baking pans. While still hot dip in butter and roll in cinnamon and sugar mixture. Serve warm.

MAKES 24

• •

Secret: These freeze well but should be frozen before the butter and sugar coatings are added. To serve, reheat puffs briefly in the microwave, dip in butter, and roll in cinnamon and sugar. They will appear to have been freshly made.

• •

Ginger Cookies

¾ cup shortening
1⅓ cups sugar
1   egg, beaten
¼ cup light molasses
2   cups all-purpose flour
¼ teaspoon salt

2   teaspoons baking soda
1   teaspoon cinnamon
1   teaspoon ginger
1   teaspoon cloves
    Granulated sugar

In a large bowl, beat shortening and sugar together with an electric mixer until smooth and creamy. Add egg and molasses and beat until incorporated.

Sift together flour, salt, baking soda, cinnamon, ginger, and cloves. Add flour mixture to butter mixture and beat until well mixed. Roll dough into a flat disc, wrap well with plastic wrap, and refrigerate for several hours or days.

Preheat oven to 350 degrees.

To make cookies, pinch off enough dough to make a ball about 1-inch in diameter. Place ball on a greased baking sheet. Flatten the dough with a flat bottom glass that has been greased and pressed in granulated sugar. Bake for 5 minutes. Remove from oven and cool on baking racks.

MAKES 6 DOZEN

Heart-Shaped Shortbread Cookies
Dipped in Chocolate

Cookies

¾ pound (3 sticks) unsalted butter at room temperature

1 cup sugar (plus extra for sprinkling)

1 teaspoon vanilla

3½ cups all-purpose flour

¼ teaspoon salt

Chocolate for Dipping

1 package (8-ounces) bittersweet chocolate

2 teaspoons peanut oil

Cookies

Preheat oven to 350 degrees.

In a large bowl, mix butter and sugar together with an electric mixer until they are just combined. Add vanilla and blend well.

In a medium bowl, sift together flour and salt. Combine flour mixture with butter and sugar mixture. Mix on low speed until dough begins to come together. When dough is ready, place on a flour dusted surface and shape into a flat disc. Cover dough with plastic wrap and refrigerate for 30 minutes.

Roll dough ½-inch thick and cut with a heart-shaped cookie cutter (or cookie cutter of your choice). Size and shape of cutter will determine amount of cookies the recipe makes. Place cookies on an ungreased baking sheet and sprinkle with sugar. Bake for 15 to 20 minutes or until edges begin to brown. After cooling, cookies may be dipped in melted chocolate to coat.

Chocolate for Dipping

Melt chocolate in a double boiler. Remove from heat and stir in peanut oil. Tilt pan to one side and dip one half of the heart-shaped cookie to cover. Let extra chocolate drip off and place cookie on wax paper to harden.

MAKES 24 HEART-SHAPED COOKIES

• •

Secret: The dipping chocolate is also wonderful for making chocolate covered strawberries.

• •

Lemon Bars

Shortbread

- 2 tablespoons powdered sugar
- 2 tablespoons granulated sugar
- 10 tablespoons cold unsalted butter, cut into 1-inch cubes
- 1¼ cups all-purpose flour

Lemon Curd

- 4 large egg yolks
- ¾ cup sugar
- 3 ounces lemon juice (about 2½ large lemons)
- 4 tablespoons unsalted butter, softened
- Pinch of salt
- 2 teaspoons lemon zest, finely grated
- 2 teaspoons powdered sugar for dusting

Shortbread

Preheat oven to 325 degrees.

Prepare an 8 x 8-inch baking pan by lining the bottom and 2 sides with heavy aluminum foil. In a food processor fitted with a metal blade, process granulated sugar and powdered sugar for 1 minute until sugar is very fine. Add cold cubed butter to sugar. Process until sugar disappears. Add flour and pulse until there are a lot of little moist crumbly pieces.

Put mixture into a plastic bag and press together. Remove dough from the plastic bag and knead it until it holds together. Pat the dough into the prepared baking pan. Use a fork to prick the dough all over. Bake for 30 to 40 minutes or until the edges are lightly browned and top is pale golden.

Lemon Curd

Place a strainer over a bowl and have it ready near the cooktop. In a heavy saucepan, beat egg yolks and sugar with a wooden spoon until well blended. Stir in lemon juice, butter, and salt. Cook over medium-low heat, stirring constantly, for about 6 minutes, until thickened and resembling hollandaise sauce. The mixture will change from translucent to opaque and begin to take on a yellow color on the back of a wooden spoon. Do not boil.

When the curd has thickened pour it into the strainer. Press through the strainer with the back of a spoon until only the coarse residue remains. Discard the residue. Stir in lemon zest.

Assembly

Lower oven temperature to 300 degrees after shortbread is done.

Pour lemon curd on top of shortbread and return to oven for 10 minutes. Cool lemon bars on a wire rack and refrigerate for 30 minutes before removing from pan. Sprinkle with powdered sugar.

To remove from pan run a knife along the unfoiled edges and use the foil to lift out the bars. Using a sharp knife cut the bars in thirds, then in half the other way, and then each half in thirds. Store in an airtight container. Keeps at room temperature 3 days, refrigerated 3 weeks, and frozen 3 months.

MAKES 18 BARS

Little Phyllo Cheesecakes

The sweet orange flavor of these miniature cheesecakes will melt in your mouth.

Phyllo Cups

12 sheets frozen phyllo pastry or 40 (3 packages) ready made phyllo cups, thawed
½ cup butter, melted

Filling

3 (3-ounce) packages cream cheese, softened
½ cup sifted powdered sugar
1½ teaspoons grated orange rind

1 tablespoon orange juice
½ cup orange marmalade
2 teaspoons orange juice

Phyllo Cups

Preheat oven to 350 degrees.

Place 1 sheet of phyllo on a cutting board (keep remaining phyllo covered with plastic wrap and a damp dishtowel). Lightly brush phyllo with melted butter. Layer 3 more sheets phyllo on first sheet, brushing each one with butter. Repeat to make 2 more stacks of phyllo. Cut each stack of phyllo into 3-inch circles using cookie cutter.

Brush miniature muffin cups with melted butter. Place a circle of layered phyllo into each muffin cup, pressing down firmly to form pastry shell. Bake for 8 to 10 minutes or until golden. Gently remove from pan, and let cool on wire racks.

Filling

Combine cream cheese, powdered sugar, orange rind, and 1 tablespoon orange juice in a small mixing bowl. Beat together with an electric mixer until creamy and smooth. Spoon 1½ teaspoons cream cheese mixture into each pastry shell.

Combine orange marmalade and 2 teaspoons orange juice. Top each cheesecake with ½ teaspoon orange marmalade mixture. Refrigerate until ready to serve.

MAKES 40

• •

Secrets: Phyllo shells may be made up to 2 days in advance and kept in an airtight container. Fill shells up to 4 hours in advance and chill until ready to serve. Make it easy and buy ready made phyllo cups in the frozen food section of the grocery store.

• •

Miniature Cream Puffs

*We like to make these cream puffs for our parties. They become
bite-size desserts or hors d'oeuvres. They are easy to make and keep well.*

1 cup water	¼ teaspoon salt
½ cup (1 stick) butter	4 eggs
1 cup all-purpose flour	

Preheat oven to 400 degrees.

Put water in a small, heavy saucepan. Cut butter into small pieces and add to water. Bring water to a boil and melt butter. Add flour and salt all at once, stirring vigorously. Cook and stir until mixture forms a ball that is smooth and does not separate. The bottom of the pan should be coated with a thin film. This indicates that the flour is cooked. Remove from heat and cool slightly.

Add eggs, one at a time, beating after each until mixture is smooth. Drop dough the size of walnuts onto a greased cookie sheet. Bake for 30 minutes. Remove from oven.

Pierce each puff in the side with a sharp knife. This allows the steam to escape and they will not become soggy. Turn oven off and put cream puffs back in to dry for 5 minutes. Remove from oven and cool on racks. Store in an airtight container and refrigerate. They will keep for a week in the refrigerator and 6 months in the freezer.

MAKES 10

For a sweet dessert puff, when making cream puffs add
½ teaspoon sugar at the same time you add the salt. After cream puffs
have cooled, cut the tops off, fill with your favorite preserves, and top with
whipped cream. For an easy savory hors d'oeuvre puff, add ½ teaspoon dill at
the same time you add the salt. When cooled, cut the tops off and fill with
smoked fish spread. Use your imagination for other combinations.

Pecan Phyllo Crisps

1 cup pecans, toasted lightly and cooled
1 cup granulated sugar
12 (17 x 12-inch) phyllo sheets, thawed

¾ cup (1½ sticks) unsalted butter, melted
Powdered sugar

Preheat oven to 350 degrees.

In a food processor fitted with a steel blade, grind toasted pecans with granulated sugar until a fine consistency is reached. Do not over process. (Pecan sugar may be made 2 days ahead and kept in an airtight container at room temperature.)

When working with phyllo, it is important to keep unused dough covered with plastic wrap and a damp dishtowel until you are ready to use. On a smooth, dry work surface, lay out 1 phyllo sheet and brush with melted butter. Sprinkle sheet evenly with about 2 tablespoons of pecan sugar. Top the sheet with another 5 phyllo sheets, brushing and sprinkling each with butter and pecan sugar. Do the same with the second set of 6 phyllo sheets. Trim the edges of stacked phyllo if uneven and cut into 48 rectangles each about 4 x 2-inches. (Cut stacked phyllo lengthwise into 3 strips and cut each crosswise into eighths.) Cut each rectangle diagonally to form 2 triangles for a total of 96 cookies.

Arrange triangles, sugared side up, in one layer on heavy baking sheets. Place baking sheets in the middle of the oven and bake 10 to 15 minutes or until golden brown. Transfer crisps to racks and cool. Sprinkle crisps with powdered sugar. Store crisps in an airtight container, at room temperature for 4 days.

MAKES 96 CRISPS

• •

Secret: These light-as-air delights are equally
delicious using almonds or walnuts in place of pecans.

• •

Toffee Brownies

This whole recipe is a secret! No one will guess it came from a simple mix.

1 package (family size) brownie mix for a
9 x 13-inch pan
Coffee, to replace water in recipe

Butter, to replace oil in recipe
3 large (6-ounce) toffee bars (Hershey
Symphony)

Follow directions on brownie mix package substituting coffee for water and butter for oil. To assemble brownies, pour ½ of the batter into a 9 x 13-inch pan. Lay toffee bars on top and then cover with remaining batter. Bake as directed on package.

MAKES APPROXIMATELY 20

Almond Tart with Fresh Berries

This is an awesome tart that is simple to make. It serves as a wonderful base
for a variety of toppings. Try it with ice cream and chocolate sauce or caramel sauce.

Almond Tart

¾	cup butter, melted	1	tablespoon almond extract
1½	cups sugar	1-2	tablespoons granulated sugar
2	eggs	1	(2-ounce) package slivered almonds
1⅓	cups flour		

Fresh Berries

2	pints fresh strawberries, hulled and cut in half	½-1	cup granulated sugar, depending on the sweetness of the berries
1	pint fresh blueberries		Vanilla ice cream
1	pint fresh raspberries		

Almond Tart

Preheat oven to 350 degrees.

Line a 10-inch cast iron skillet with foil and butter the foil. In a large bowl, beat butter and sugar together with an electric mixer until well blended. Beat in eggs, one at a time until smooth and creamy. Mix in flour, a little at a time. Finally, add almond extract, mixing well.

Transfer mixture to the prepared iron skillet, and sprinkle with granulated sugar and slivered almonds. Bake for 45 minutes or until golden. When finished baking, remove from skillet immediately and let cool in foil.

Fresh Berries

Gently wash and dry berries. Mix berries with sugar and refrigerate. May be prepared a day ahead.

Assembly

Slice tart into wedges and top with vanilla ice cream and fresh berries.

SERVES 8 TO 10

Chocolate Truffle Tart
with Pecan-Caramel Sauce

Don't be put off by this long recipe. It is the
ultimate chocolate experience and well worth the effort.

Crust

1⅔ cups all-purpose flour
⅓ cup cocoa powder
¾ cup powdered sugar
1   teaspoon vanilla

½ teaspoon ground cinnamon
½ teaspoon salt
1   cup unsalted butter

Filling

½ cup unsalted butter
1   pound (16-ounces) bittersweet
     chocolate, cut into pieces
½ cup sugar

4   eggs
1   teaspoon vanilla
1   heaping tablespoon instant espresso
     powder

Pecan-Caramel Sauce

1   cup sugar
⅓ cup water
½ coarsely chopped pecans
⅓ cup light corn syrup

½ cup good heavy whipping cream
¼ cup dark rum
2   tablespoons unsalted butter

Garnish

1   cup heavy whipping cream, whipped or
     scoops of vanilla ice cream

Fresh mint leaves

Crust

Preheat oven to 350 degrees.

Butter a 10-inch flan or tart pan with a removable bottom and set aside. Put flour, cocoa, powdered sugar, vanilla, cinnamon, and salt in the bowl of a food processor fitted with the steel blade. With the machine running, add butter about 1 tablespoon at a time, through the feeder tube. Process until dough collects on top of the blade. Remove dough and press into prepared pan. Bake in oven for about 10 minutes or just until the dough is set. Remove from oven and let crust cool. Do not turn off oven.

Filling

Put butter and half the chocolate pieces in top of a double boiler over gently simmering water. Melt chocolate completely. Remove bowl from heat and stir in sugar and eggs. Mix well. Add remaining chocolate pieces, vanilla, and espresso powder mixing well. Pour filling into prepared crust and bake for about 30 minutes or just until the middle is set.

Pecan-Caramel Sauce

Place sugar in a large skillet and gently moisten with water. Cook over high heat for 5 to 6 minutes. Do not stir. When the caramel starts to turn golden, swirl the pan to even the color of the caramel.

Chocolate Truffle Tart with Pecan-Caramel Sauce continued

Add pecans, corn syrup, then slowly add the cream. Cook until the sugar dissolves and the sauce starts to thicken, about 3 to 5 minutes. Add rum and butter and cook until butter is melted, about 1 minute. Remove pan from heat and let sauce cool for about 15 minutes. (If you make the sauce ahead, reheat it before serving.)

Assembly

Slice the tart while still warm. Pour some of the warm Pecan-Caramel Sauce over each slice, top with a dollop of whipped cream or a scoop of vanilla ice cream, garnish with a mint sprig, and serve.

SERVES 8 TO 10

• •

Secret: For the Special Occasion Reception make recipe 7 times.

• •

Coconut Cream Miniature Tarts

2 cups whole milk	1 teaspoon vanilla
1 cup sugar	1 (3.5 ounce) can coconut flakes
⅓ cup flour	3-4 packages (15 cups per package) frozen
Pinch of salt	phyllo cups, thawed
3 egg yolks	

Heat milk in a large heavy saucepan over medium-low heat to just below the boiling point. (Tiny bubbles will form at the edges of the milk.)

In a medium bowl, mix together sugar, flour, salt, and egg yolks. If the egg yolks are small, add a little milk to make a creamy consistency. Pour flour mixture into hot milk and cook and stir until thick, about 10 minutes. Add vanilla and beat with a wire whisk until a creamy consistency. Add coconut and mix well. Press wax paper or plastic wrap directly onto the surface of coconut cream and refrigerate until ready to use. Fill phyllo cups just before serving.

MAKES APPROXIMATELY 50 TARTS

• •

Secret: Frozen phyllo cups may be purchased in the frozen food section of the grocery store.

• •

> **Y**ou may also make this into a traditional pie by filling your favorite baked and cooled 9-inch pie crust. To prevent skin from forming on surface of filling, put wax paper directly on top of hot filling, then refrigerate. When ready to serve top with whipped cream.

Freeze-Ahead Key Lime Pie

Crumb Crust
1¼ cups graham cracker crumbs
5 tablespoons butter or margarine

¼ cup sugar
1 teaspoon cinnamon

Key Lime Filling
4 egg yolks, beaten
1 can sweetened condensed milk

½ cup fresh Florida lime juice

Crumb Crust
Combine crumbs, butter, sugar and cinnamon. Press crumb mixture over the bottom and up the side of a 9-inch pie plate. Bake at 350 degrees for 8 minutes or until golden brown. Let stand until cool.

Key Lime Filling
In a medium bowl, whisk together beaten egg yolks, condensed milk, and lime juice. Spoon filling into prepared pie plate and freeze until firm. Before serving, allow pie to stand at room temperature for 15 minutes.

SERVES 8 TO 10

• •

Secret: If you have concerns about raw eggs, combine yolks with ½ cup of lime juice (used in the recipe) in double boiler. Whisk constantly over medium heat until mixture reaches 140 degrees; do not boil.

• •

We served these as miniature tarts at one of our first Silver Coffee parties back in the early eighties. Instead of using a 9-inch pie pan, press crumb mixture into miniature tart pans, bake, and fill with Key Lime Filling. These are nice served at a ladies' coffee or tea.

Lemon Buttermilk Tart

Pleasingly creamy with just a little pucker.

Lemon Crust
1 cup flaked coconut
½ cup gingersnap crumbs
½ cup graham cracker crumbs

¼ cup (½ stick) butter, melted
2 tablespoons flour

Lemon Buttermilk Filling
¼ cup buttermilk
½ cup sugar
2 large eggs

5 tablespoons fresh lemon juice
2 tablespoons flour
½ teaspoon grated lemon rind

Lemon Crust
Preheat oven to 350 degrees.

Mix coconut, gingersnap crumbs, graham cracker crumbs, butter, and flour together. Firmly press into a 9-inch pie plate. Bake for 5 minutes. Refrigerate until ready to fill with lemon filling.

Lemon Buttermilk Filling
Preheat oven to 350 degrees.

Whisk buttermilk, sugar, eggs, lemon juice, flour, and lemon rind in a medium bowl to blend. Pour into lemon crust. Bake about 30 minutes, or until filling is set. Cool completely. Refrigerate until cold.

SERVES 8

• •

Secret: For the Book Club Luncheon make 2 pies or use miniature tart variation.

• •

This recipe can be adapted to make miniature tarts. Press the lemon crust into miniature muffin pans. Bake crusts for 5 minutes at 350 degrees. Spoon lemon filling into each tart. Return to oven and bake until filling is set. Cool 5 to 10 minutes and carefully remove tarts and store in refrigerator until ready to serve.

MAKES 24 TARTS

Mango-Pineapple Tart
with Macadamia Nut Crust

Macadamia Nut Crust

1½ cups all-purpose flour
1 cup Macadamia nuts
½ cup sugar
¼ teaspoon salt

10 tablespoons (1¼ sticks) unsalted butter,
   chilled and cut into ½-inch slices
1 large egg yolk
1 teaspoon water
½ teaspoon almond extract

Custard Filling

1½ cups whole milk
½ cup whipping cream
1 vanilla bean, split lengthwise
6 large egg yolks

½ cup sugar
¼ cup cornstarch
3½ teaspoons dark rum

Fruit Filling

½ pineapple, halved lengthwise, cored,
   and cut crosswise into ¼-inch thick
   slices

2 mangoes, peeled, halved, and cut
   crosswise into ¼-inch thick slices
¼ cup apricot preserves, melted

Macadamia Nut Crust

Place flour, Macadamia nuts, sugar, and salt in a food processor fitted with the steel blade. Using the pulse button, turn on and off until nuts are finely ground. Add butter slices. Using the pulse button, turn on and off, until pea-size pieces form. Add yolk, 1 teaspoon water and extract. Using the pulse button, turn on and off and blend until moist clumps form. Add more water by teaspoonfuls if dough is dry. Gather into a ball and flatten into disk. Wrap in plastic wrap and refrigerate 3 hours.

When well chilled, roll out dough between 2 lightly floured sheets of waxed paper to ¼-inch thickness. Peel off top sheet of paper. Invert crust into 11-inch round tart pan with removable bottom. Peel off paper, press dough into pan and trim edges. Push crust ⅛-inch above the top edge of pan. Refrigerate 1 hour.

Preheat oven to 375 degrees.

Bake crust until golden, about 25 minutes. Cool. (Can be made 1 day ahead. Wrap in plastic wrap and store at room temperature.)

Custard Filling

In a medium saucepan, combine milk and cream over medium heat. Scrape in seeds from vanilla bean and add whole bean. Bring milk mixture to a simmer.

Mango-Pineapple Tart with Macadamia Nut Crust continued

In a large bowl, whisk together yolks, sugar, and cornstarch, blending well. Gradually whisk hot milk mixture into yolk mixture and return to saucepan. Whisk over medium heat until thick and beginning to bubble, about 5 minutes. Cool slightly and mix in rum. Transfer to a medium bowl, and press plastic wrap onto surface of custard. Refrigerate until cool, at least 4 hours. (Can be made 1 day ahead. Keep refrigerated.)

Fruit Filling and Assembly

Remove vanilla bean from custard filling. Whisk custard just until smooth and creamy and spread in crust. Prepare pineapple and mango slices and arrange in concentric circles on top of filling. Brush fruit with preserves. (Tart can be assembled 3 hours ahead. Refrigerate until ready to serve.)

SERVES 12

Peppermint Ice Cream Pie

This is a crowd-pleasing dessert. It's perfect to serve at Christmas time.

2   (1-ounce) squares semisweet chocolate
½   cup butter
2   large eggs
1   cup sugar
½   cup all-purpose flour
⅛   teaspoon salt

1   quart peppermint stick ice cream, softened
½   cup hot fudge sauce (may purchase)
2   cups whipping cream
½   cup finely crushed hard peppermint
      candies
      Hard peppermint candies, for garnish

Preheat oven to 350 degrees.

Grease and flour a 10-inch pie plate. Melt chocolate and butter in a saucepan over medium-low heat, stirring occasionally. Set aside to cool.

Using an electric mixer set at medium speed, beat eggs in a large bowl until slightly thickened. Gradually add sugar, beating well. Combine flour and salt and add to eggs along with cooled chocolate mixture. Beat just until blended. Spread batter evenly into the prepared pie plate. Bake for 30 to 35 minutes or until done. Allow to cool completely.

Spoon ice cream into pie crust, and freeze 1 hour. Drizzle fudge sauce over ice cream and swirl gently with a knife. Freeze 2 to 3 hours or until firm.

Beat whipping cream until soft peaks form. Gently fold in crushed peppermint candies. Pipe or spoon whipped cream over frozen pie. Return to freezer for 30 minutes. When ready to serve, let pie stand at room temperature for 5 to 10 minutes before slicing. If desired, garnish with hard peppermint candies.

SERVES 8 TO 10

• •
Secret: For the Holiday Cocktail Buffet make 8 to 9 pies.
• •

Tiny Glazed Fruit Tarts

*This simple yet elegant custard is a versatile performer. It can be spooned
directly into pudding dishes or piped into chocolate eclairs. It can be combined with coconut
or chocolate to make delicious pie fillings. It is used here as the base for tiny fruit tarts.*

Custard

4 cups whole milk	Pinch salt
2 cups sugar	6 whole eggs, beaten
⅔ cup flour	2 teaspoons vanilla

Fruit and Glaze

2-4 pints unblemished strawberries,   2 (12-ounce) jars red raspberry or red
    raspberries, blueberries, pitted grapes,   currant jelly
    or fruit of your choice   4 tablespoons orange flavored liqueur

Custard

Heat milk in a heavy saucepan over medium-low heat, just to the boiling point (steam will start to rise when ready).

In a large bowl, combine sugar, flour, and salt. Blend beaten eggs into dry ingredients, mixing thoroughly. Beat egg mixture into hot milk. Cook custard mixture over low heat, stirring constantly with a wooden spoon, scraping the bottom and sides of the pan until custard becomes thick, about 5 minutes. Be careful not to allow mixture to boil. Remove from heat and blend in vanilla with a whisk. Allow custard to cool. Whisk custard several times as it is cooling to keep the texture creamy.

When custard is completely cooled, fill toast cups or transfer to a plastic container, press plastic wrap directly onto the surface and refrigerate until needed.

MAKES ENOUGH CUSTARD FOR TWO 9-INCH PIES OR 100 TARTS

Fruit and Glaze

Wash fruit individually in cheap white wine and pat dry. Fruit prepared this way will keep for several days in the refrigerator. Melt liqueur and jelly together in a small saucepan and set glaze aside.

Tart Assembly

100 toast cups (recipe follows) or use   1 recipe custard filling
    purchased pastry cups (thinnest is   Fruit and glaze
    best)

Arrange toast cups on a baking sheet, place a teaspoon of custard in each toast cup, and top with a piece of fruit. If the fruit is too large, cut it in half. Using a small brush, paint a bit of glaze over the fruit. This final assembly should be done only at the last minute.

MAKES 100 TINY TARTS (YOU MAY HAVE SOME CUSTARD LEFT OVER)

Tiny Glazed Fruit Tarts continued

• •

Secrets: The custard will keep for 2 days. The fruit can be prepared a day or two in advance. Remember, however, that the tarts should be put together as late as possible to make sure that the crusts don't get soggy and the glaze doesn't run. The use of whole milk is critical to the success of the custard. It is also extremely important to whisk the mixture as it is cooling. You are always wise to make the initial custard very thick, since it is difficult to thicken when already made, but very easily thinned after cooking by adding more milk or cream.

• •

When preparing the custard to fill 9-inch pies, separate eggs and add yolks to sugar and flour mixture as outlined in the master recipe. Use the reserved egg whites for meringue. Beat egg whites with ¼ teaspoon cream of tartar until soft peaks form. Gradually add 4 tablespoons of sugar, beating until stiff and glossy peaks form and all sugar is dissolved. Spread meringue over custard filling, sealing to edge of pastry. Bake at 350 degrees for 12 minutes, or until meringue is golden.

MAKES ENOUGH FOR 2 (9-INCH) PIES

Toast Cups

These make great containers for all kinds of little bites, from savories to sweets. If time is a factor, don't hesitate to substitute store bought pastry cups or frozen phyllo cups. While time consuming, toast cups are the most economical.

4   loaves of the absolute cheapest, freshest white bread
1   pound (4 sticks) margarine

Preheat oven to 300 degrees.

Melt margarine and pour into a shallow bowl. Using a 2¾-inch scalloped cookie cutter, cut one round from each slice of bread. Dip one round into the melted butter on one side only. Press another bread round against the buttered side of the first round. Using your fingers, gently press the two rounds together on waxed paper until they are doughy and about as thin as crêpes.

Carefully pull bread scallops apart and gently fit into miniature muffin pans, dry side down. Place in oven and toast for 5 to 10 minutes or until golden. Store at room temperature in an airtight container. These will keep for several days. Do not freeze.

MAKES 100

• •

Secret: We've found that old wine corks are useful aids in pressing the bread into the miniature muffin pans.

• •

*T*he toast cups have been our special secret for many years. They look fabulous and, when baked correctly, taste great also. While they may be tedious if you are working alone, they are great fun as a project among friends. The secret for making the crusts is to be sure that you have muffin pans and cutters of the correct size. After experimenting, we found an inexpensive scalloped cookie cutter, measuring 2¾-inches scallop to scallop, to be the perfect size for our miniature muffin pans. If you cannot locate the right equipment, or for variety's sake would prefer another shape, you might try making handkerchief shells. Cut each slice of bread into 2½-inch squares. Continue as in master recipe. When placing squares into the miniature muffin pans, gently press pulling opposite corners up into points as you would to stuff a handkerchief into a breast pocket. Toast as in the master recipe.

Chocolate Sin Cake

The biggest sin is having to give away the leftovers because you can't stop eating it!

1 pound semisweet chocolate, chopped	4 tablespoons granulated sugar, divided
8 tablespoons (1 stick) unsalted butter, cut into tablespoons, at room temperature	1 tablespoon cornstarch
	2 teaspoons vanilla
4 large eggs, separated	¼ teaspoon cream of tartar
	Powdered sugar for topping

Preheat oven to 350 degrees.

Butter a 10-inch springform pan, and sprinkle with granulated sugar. Melt chocolate in top of a double boiler over simmering water. When chocolate has completely melted, whisk in butter, 1 tablespoon at a time. Let mixture cool slightly.

Using an electric mixer on high speed, beat egg yolks with 2 tablespoons of granulated sugar in a medium bowl. Continue beating until the mixture is ivory colored and as thick as marshmallow topping, about 5 minutes. Stir in cornstarch and vanilla. Set egg mixture aside.

In a medium bowl, using an electric mixer, beat egg whites, adding cream of tartar after 20 seconds. Add remaining 2 tablespoons sugar as the whites stiffen to soft peaks. Fold reserved egg yolk mixture into cooled chocolate mixture. Finally, fold in egg whites as gently as possible.

Spoon batter into the prepared pan. Bake cake about 30 minutes or until firm on top, although the center will be a little soft. Remove cake from the oven and set on a wire rack. Let cake cool to room temperature. Run a knife around the inside edge of the pan and remove sides. The cake will sink a little in the center. Dust the top of the cake with powdered sugar using a doily to make a decorative pattern. Carefully slide the cake onto a serving platter using a large spatula.

SERVES 8 TO 10

Pineapple Upside-Down Cake

⅓ cup butter	⅔ cup sugar
½ cup packed brown sugar	6 tablespoons pineapple juice
8 slices (20-ounce can) pineapple, drained	1 teaspoon vanilla
Maraschino cherries	1 cup sifted flour
Pecan halves	⅓ teaspoon baking powder
2 eggs	¼ teaspoon salt

Preheat oven to 350 degrees.

Melt butter in a 10-inch skillet or baking pan. Sprinkle brown sugar evenly over butter. Arrange pineapple slices on brown sugar, center with cherries, and place pecans between slices. Set aside.

Using an electric mixer, beat eggs until thick and lemon-colored. Add sugar gradually, followed by pineapple juice and vanilla. In a medium bowl, sift together flour, baking powder, and salt. Beat dry ingredients into egg mixture all at once. Pour batter over pineapple slices and bake for 45 minutes or until cake tests done. Cool for 5 minutes, invert onto a serving plate, and serve warm.

SERVES 9

• •

Secret: For the Special Occasion Reception make recipe 7 times.

• •

Candied Citrus Peel

8 grapefruits or 16 oranges (select fruit with a thick, unblemished skin)	1 gallon water
5 cups granulated sugar, divided	2 cups superfine sugar

Cut citrus into quarters and remove flesh, leaving as much white membrane as possible attached to the skin. Reserve the fruit for another use. Place the citrus peels in a large pot and cover with cold water. Bring water to a boil and boil for about a minute. Pour peels into a colander, rinse under cold water. Cut peels into lengthwise strips ¼-inch wide.

In a large container, mix together 1 gallon water and 3 cups granulated sugar. Add to the cooking pot along with the citrus peels. Bring to a boil and boil gently, uncovered, for about 1½ hours. The skins should become almost transparent and there should be just enough thick syrup to cover them.

Dredge peels in a mixture of 2 cups superfine sugar and remaining 2 cups granulated sugar. Arrange in a single layer on racks to cool, dry, and harden completely. Store in an airtight container.

MAKES ABOUT 12 DOZEN

• •

Secret: Superfine sugar can be purchased at a specialty food store, or made by whirling granulated sugar in a food processor, fitted with a steel blade.

• •

Sweets

Pralines

These are the real deal. For an easier praline try the microwave variation.

3 cups granulated sugar
1½ cups milk
3 cups pecans, chopped

1 large cooking spoon (approximately ⅛ cup) white Karo syrup
2 tablespoons butter
1 teaspoon vanilla

Cook sugar, milk, pecans, and Karo syrup together to soft-ball stage (234 degrees). Set aside to cool (approximately 15 minutes). Add butter and vanilla. Whip mixture using a heavy stainless steel spoon until smooth and creamy (less than 5 minutes). The minute the mixture turns creamy, turn out by spoonfuls onto parchment paper or wax paper. Let pralines cool and harden.

MAKES 2 DOZEN

Microwave Pralines

This Silver Sister's grandmother would turn over in her grave if she knew she used this easy recipe.

2 cups brown sugar
½ pint whipping cream

2 tablespoons melted butter
1 cup pecan halves

Stir together brown sugar and whipping cream. Microwave on high for 13 minutes non-stop. Immediately stir in the melted butter and pecan halves. Spoon out onto wax paper to cool and harden.

MAKES 3 TO 4 DOZEN

Ice Cream Sandwiches

A great little treat to have in your freezer. These were a huge hit at a recent night time party. Use any kind of homemade or purchased cookie with any flavor ice cream. Be creative!

72 (2-inch) Ginger Cookies (see index)   **1   quart lemon ice cream**

Bake Ginger Cookies, making them 2-inches in diameter. Soften ice cream in jelly-roll pan, spread evenly, and refreeze. When frozen, cut ice cream into 2-inch rounds using a 2-inch round cookie cutter. Place an ice cream round on underside of cookie and top with another cookie.

Immediately return ice cream sandwich to freezer. Work quickly, as ice cream will melt making it difficult to work with.

MAKES 36

Stepping Out
"Rave Faves"

The Silver Sisters who love to cook
share their personal favorite recipes.

Sponsored by
Marilyn and John Connelly

Stepping Out ~ "Rave Faves"

Ahi Ceviche

¾ pound (12-ounces) trimmed fresh tuna
   (ahi), cubed
  Juice of 6 limes
  Juice of 6 lemons
1 Habenero chili, diced
1 orange, juiced and sectioned into cubes

Fresh mint, chopped
Fresh basil, chopped
Fresh cilantro, chopped
Salt, to taste
Freshly ground black pepper, to taste

Combine tuna, lime juice, lemon juice, Habenero chili, orange juice and cubes, mint, basil, cilantro, salt, and pepper in a non-reactive pan and marinate for 1 hour. Discard juice and serve with homemade pita crisps or tortilla chips.

SERVES 8 AS AN HORS D'OEUVRE

• •

Secret: This serves 4 if used as a first course.

• •

Best-Ever Deviled Eggs

6 eggs, hard-boiled, cooled and halved
   lengthwise
½ cup Mom's dressing

¼ cup grainy mustard
1 tablespoon mayonnaise
  Salt and pepper, to taste

Mom's Dressing

1 cup sugar
2 beaten eggs

1 cup white vinegar

Mom's Dressing

Combine sugar, beaten eggs, and white vinegar in a medium saucepan. Cook and stir over medium heat until sugar is dissolved and dressing is as thick as egg-based commercial salad dressing. Transfer dressing to an airtight container and store in the refrigerator. It will keep for a month, at least.

Assembly

Remove the yolks from the hard-boiled eggs. Place yolks in a medium bowl and mash thoroughly. Mix in Mom's dressing, mustard, and mayonnaise and blend until smooth. Add salt and pepper to taste. Mound the mixture back into the halved egg whites. Refrigerate until served.

MAKES 12 EGGS

• •

Secret: Mom's Dressing is wonderful as a base for pimento cheese spread. Add good grated sharp cheese, a little yellow mustard, along with pimentos. Mix together until well combined.

• •

Creamy Clam Dip

1 (8-ounce) package cream cheese, softened
¼ cup sour cream
2 (6½-ounce) cans minced clams, drained reserving 3 tablespoons liquid
⅓ cup red bell pepper, finely chopped

1 shallot, minced
2 tablespoons minced fresh parsley
¾ teaspoon Worcestershire sauce
½ teaspoon cayenne pepper
Salt

In a bowl whisk together cream cheese and sour cream until smooth. Stir in clams, red bell pepper, shallot, parsley, Worcestershire, cayenne, and salt to taste. Serve dip with toast points or chips.

MAKES ABOUT 2 CUPS

Hot Artichoke and Feta Dip with Shrimp

1 (14-ounce) can artichoke hearts, drained and chopped
2 packages crumbled basil and tomato feta cheese
1 cup mayonnaise

½ cup shredded Parmesan cheese
1 jar diced pimentos, drained
1 clove garlic, minced
½ pound of cooked shrimp, chopped (optional)

Preheat oven to 350 degrees. Mix together artichokes, feta, mayonnaise, Parmesan, pimentos, garlic, and shrimp. Pour into a 9-inch round pie plate. Bake for 20 to 25 minutes or until bubbly.

SERVES 15

Lazy Day Shrimp Delight

2 (8-ounce) packages cream cheese with chives, softened
1 (12-ounce) jar cocktail sauce
1½ pounds shrimp, cooked, peeled, deveined and chopped if shrimp are too large (reserve a few whole shrimp for garnish)

1 (8-ounce) package Monterey Jack cheese, grated
4 green onions, chopped
½ green bell pepper, chopped
½ cup ripe sliced olives (optional)
1 tomato, chopped
1 squeeze fresh lime juice

Spread cream cheese on a serving platter. Top with cocktail sauce, shrimp, cheese, green onions, bell pepper, olives, and tomato, in that order. Squeeze lime juice over mixture. Decorate with a few whole shrimp. Serve with Melba rounds or other favorite crackers.

SERVES 15

Olive Nut Cheese Spread

1 (8-ounce) package cream cheese,
     softened
¾ cup good mayonnaise
     Pinch cayenne pepper

1½ cups chopped olives (salad olives),
     drained well
1 cup finely chopped pecans

In a medium bowl, mix together cream cheese, mayonnaise, and cayenne. Add olives and pecans to cheese mixture, blending well. Cover mixture and refrigerate at least an hour. When ready to serve, place on a plate, forming into a mound. Serve with crackers.

MAKES 1 CHEESE BALL

Rosemary Cheese Mold

1 (8-ounce) package cream cheese, softened
1 (3-ounce) package goat cheese, softened
1 tablespoon fresh chopped rosemary
2 teaspoons honey

1 teaspoon coarse pepper
     Cooking spray
     Fig preserves

In a food processor fitted with the steel blade, mix cream cheese, goat cheese, rosemary, honey and pepper until smooth. Grease a mini Bundt pan (1½-cup size) using cooking spray, line with plastic wrap and grease wrap, using cooking spray. Spoon cheese mixture into prepared pan and refrigerate for 2 hours. Carefully remove cheese from pan and place on a serving plate. Top with fig preserves and serve with water crackers.

SERVES 8

Salami Crisps

These are deceptively simple and incredibly yummy.

24 paper-thin slices (4-inch rounds) Genoa salami (¼-pound)

Put oven racks in upper and lower thirds of oven and preheat oven to 325 degrees. Line 2 large baking sheets with parchment paper. Arrange salami slices in 1 layer on sheets. Bake, switching position of baking sheets halfway through baking, about 10 to 15 minutes. When finished edges should be crisp and begin to curl. Transfer to a rack to cool. They will crisp as they cool.

MAKES 24

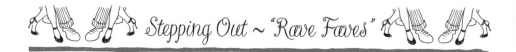

Walnut, Arugula, and Gorgonzola Crostini

Butter, room temperature	1 (4-ounce) package crumbled
14 (¼-inch) thick diagonal baguette bread	Gorgonzola cheese
slices	3 tablespoons finely chopped arugula
6 tablespoons chopped toasted walnuts	Freshly ground black pepper
	Arugula leaves

Preheat oven to 400 degrees.

Spread butter over one side of each baguette slice. Arrange slices on baking sheet, butter side up. Bake until golden, about 8 to 10 minutes. Cool and set aside.

Reduce oven temperature to 350 degrees. Mix walnuts, Gorgonzola, and arugula in a medium bowl. Spoon nut-cheese mixture evenly over baguette toasts, pressing to adhere. Season toasts with pepper. Bake toasts just until cheese melts, about 6 minutes. Cool crostini slightly. Arrange on a serving platter and garnish with arugula leaves.

MAKES 14 SLICES

Lentil Stew

This is a great cold weather, vegetarian, one-dish meal. Serve with a crusty wedge of bread.

2 tablespoons olive oil	1 (28-ounce) can plum tomatoes,
2 cups coarsely chopped onion	chopped, with their juices
2 cups chopped carrots (½-inch pieces)	1 tablespoon brown sugar
1 tablespoon minced garlic	1 cinnamon stick
2 teaspoons ground cumin	½ cup flat-leaf parsley (optional)
1 cup dried lentils, rinsed	Salt and freshly ground black pepper, to
4 cups chicken broth	taste

Heat oil in a large, heavy pot over medium-low heat. Add onions and carrots, and cook for 8 minutes, stirring occasionally. Add garlic and cook 2 minutes longer. Add cumin and cook 1 minute longer. Add the lentils, chicken broth, tomatoes and their juices, brown sugar and cinnamon stick. Bring mixture to a boil, reduce heat slightly, cover partially, and cook for 45 minutes, stirring occasionally. Stir in parsley, if desired, and season to taste with salt and pepper. Serve in shallow bowls.

SERVES 6

Cream of Cauliflower Soup

Don't even think about using low-fat nonfat anything. Reduced fat sour cream is okay.

2	tablespoons vegetable oil		Bouquet garni (½ teaspoon peppercorns, 1 teaspoon tarragon, 1 bay leaf)
½	cup chopped onion	½	stick butter
1	carrot, peeled and grated	¾	cup flour
2	cups chopped celery	2	cups milk (whole milk)
3	heads cauliflower (about 1 pound), cut into florets	1	cup half-and-half
4	tablespoons dried parsley or (2 tablespoons fresh, chopped)	2	tablespoons salt or to taste
8	cups (64-ounces) chicken broth (purchased)	1	cup sour cream

Heat oil in 8 to 10 quart stockpot over medium heat. Add onion and sauté until transparent, stirring frequently. Add carrot and celery and cook 2 minutes, stirring frequently. Add cauliflower and parsley. Cover, reduce heat to low and cook 15 minutes, stirring occasionally to prevent sticking. Add chicken stock and bouquet garni and bring to a boil over medium heat. Reduce heat and simmer 5 minutes.

Melt butter in 2 quart saucepan. Stir in flour to make a roux. Slowly add milk, whisking constantly to blend. Bring mixture to boil over medium heat, stirring frequently, until mixture is thick and smooth, (about the thickness of pudding). This will happen quickly.

Remove from heat and stir in half-and-half. Stir mixture into simmering soup. Season to taste with salt and simmer gently for about 15 to 20 minutes. Just before serving, mix a few tablespoons of soup with sour cream. Stir sour cream mixture into soup. Reheat and serve.

SERVES 8 TO 10

Escarole Soup

1	pound sweet Italian sausage, casing removed	1	(46 ounce) can chicken broth
1	medium onion, chopped	1	head escarole, cleaned and coarsely chopped
1	large clove garlic, crushed	1	cup uncooked small pasta (stars, alphabets, etc.)
1	(28 ounce) can whole tomatoes, quartered	1	(16-ounce) can cannellini beans

In a large stockpot over medium heat, brown sausage, breaking it up with a spoon. Add onion and garlic and cook for 3 minutes. Stir in tomatoes and their liquid. Stir in broth. Bring to a boil, and add escarole. Simmer soup, covered, about 15 minutes.

While soup is simmering, cook pasta as directed and drain. Rinse beans thoroughly and drain. Add pasta and beans to soup and heat through. It is best made one day ahead.

SERVES 12

Spanish Black Bean Soup

1	pound dry black beans	1	clove garlic, finely chopped
½	gallon water	3	bay leaves
1	small ham hock (or left over ham)	3	teaspoons salt
¼	cup olive oil	½	cup vinegar
2	large onions, chopped		White rice
1	green bell pepper, chopped		Onion, finely chopped

Wash beans well and soak overnight in ½ gallon water. Place beans with their soaking water in a stockpot. Add ham hock and bring to a boil, then reduce heat to simmer.

Heat olive oil in a medium skillet over medium-high heat. Add onions, green bell peppers, and garlic and cook until softened, about 10 minutes.

Add mixture to beans along with bay leaves and salt. Cook over low heat until beans are tender and the liquid is a thick consistency. (Cook slowly, as it burns easily.) Just before serving add vinegar. Serve over rice, topped with chopped onion.

SERVES 6 TO 8

Turkey Vegetable Soup

1	(10-ounce) package frozen chopped spinach	1	cup thinly sliced celery
¼	cup (½ stick) butter	1	tablespoon dried parsley (or 2 tablespoons fresh)
2	medium onions, chopped	¼-½	teaspoon sage
2	tablespoons all-purpose flour (whole wheat)	2	cups cubed cooked turkey (or chicken)
1	teaspoon curry powder	1½	cups half-and-half
3	cups chicken broth		Salt, to taste
1	cup thinly sliced carrots		Freshly ground black pepper, to taste

Thaw spinach and squeeze out all the water. This is very important.

Melt butter in large saucepan over medium-high heat. Add onions and sauté until translucent and limp, about 10 minutes. Stir in flour and curry and cook about 3 minutes. This is very important so flour doesn't taste "raw". Add broth, carrots, celery, parsley and sage. Bring to boil. Reduce heat to low, cover and simmer 10 minutes.

Add turkey, half-and-half and spinach. Cover and continue simmering until heated through, about 7 minutes. Do not boil after half-and-half is added or the soup will curdle. Season with salt and pepper. Serve hot.

SERVES 6 TO 8

Bread Sticks

These are easy and delicious. A great item to have stored in your freezer.

12 hoagie rolls	½ cup grated Parmesan cheese
1 pound (4 sticks) butter	¼-½ teaspoon garlic salt

Preheat oven to 300 degrees.

Using a serrated bread knife, carefully slice rolls in half. Cut each half into halves lengthwise. Melt butter in a shallow bowl in the microwave. Add Parmesan and garlic salt to butter. Mix together and continue to stir frequently as you dip the roll sections in the hot mixture. Place bread sticks on cookie sheets.

Sprinkle extra Parmesan on bread sticks before baking. Bake for 15 to 20 minutes. Turn sticks over and bake for another 15 to 20 minutes (30 to 40 minutes total) or until golden and crisp. Remove from oven and cool. When cool freeze on cookie sheets before storing in zip-top plastic freezer bags in the freezer. Reheat at 325 degrees for 5 minutes.

MAKES 48

Herbed Drop Biscuits

1 cup all-purpose flour	3 tablespoons cold unsalted butter, cut into 3 pieces
½ teaspoon salt	½ cup buttermilk
½ teaspoon freshly ground black pepper	¼ cup finely chopped parsley
1 teaspoon baking powder	
1 teaspoon baking soda	

Preheat oven to 450 degrees.

In a large bowl, combine, flour, salt, pepper, baking powder, and baking soda. Mix in butter, with a pastry cutter or 2 knives until the mixture resembles coarse crumbs. (Do not over mix.)

Make a well in the center of the mixture and add buttermilk and parsley. Stir gently until just combined (the batter should be lumpy).

Using a tablespoon, drop batter onto an ungreased cookie sheet, leaving an inch between the biscuits. Bake 7 to 9 minutes or until just golden. Serve warm.

MAKES 12

• •

Secret: To change flavors use different herbs. Instead of parsley try dill, rosemary or basil.

• •

Perfect Sour Cream Muffins

Warning: these tender melt-in-your-mouth morsels are highly addictive, and too easy to make.

½ cup (1stick) unsalted butter, cold, cut
    into pieces
1 cup flour

1 teaspoon salt
1 cup sour cream

Preheat oven to 400 degrees.

Spray miniature tart pans with cooking spray. Combine flour and salt in a mixing bowl. Add butter, and working quickly, use a pastry blender or two knives to cut in the ingredients until mixture resembles coarse crumbs. Add sour cream and mix until just blended. The dough may be sticky.

Drop by spoonfuls into prepared tart pans, fill almost to the top, and bake for 12 minutes or until slightly golden. Remove from pans and serve warm.

MAKES ABOUT 24

Green Bean, Walnut, and Feta Salad

1 cup coarsely chopped walnuts
¾ cup olive oil
¼ cup white wine vinegar
1 tablespoon chopped fresh dill
½ teaspoon minced garlic

¼ teaspoon salt
¼ teaspoon pepper
1½ pounds fresh green beans
1 small purple onion, thinly sliced
1 (4-ounce) package crumbled feta cheese

Preheat oven to 350 degrees.

Bake walnuts in a shallow pan, stirring occasionally, 5 to 10 minutes or until toasted, set aside.

Mix together oil, vinegar, fresh dill, garlic, salt, and pepper. Store in an airtight container and refrigerate.

Cut green beans into thirds, cook in a pot of boiling water until crisp-tender, about 8 minutes. Immediately plunge green beans into ice water to stop cooking process. Drain and pat dry.

Combine walnuts, beans, onion, and cheese in a large bowl. Pour oil mixture over bean mixture and carefully toss. Cover and refrigerate.

SERVES 6

Crunchy Broccoli Salad

Salad Dressing

⅓ cup mayonnaise (may use low-fat)
½ cup plain yogurt (may use nonfat)

¼ cup sugar
2 tablespoons vinegar

Broccoli Salad

1 large bunch fresh broccoli, chopped into bite-size pieces
1 small red onion, thinly sliced

4 strips bacon, cooked crisp and crumbled
½ cup raisins
½ cup chopped walnuts

Salad Dressing

Stir together mayonnaise, yogurt, sugar, and vinegar. Cover and refrigerate until ready to use.

Assembly

Mix together broccoli, onion, bacon, raisins, and walnuts. Pour salad dressing over broccoli mixture and toss to combine.

SERVES 8

Layered Potato Salad

Salad

8 medium potatoes, peeled
1 cup chopped fresh parsley

2 onions, minced

Dressing

1½ cups mayonnaise
1 cup sour cream
1½ teaspoons horseradish

½ teaspoon salt
1 teaspoon celery seed

Salad

Cook potatoes in boiling water until done, about 15 to 20 minutes. Drain and cool slightly. Slice potatoes ⅛ to ¼-inch thick. Mix together parsley and onion. Set aside.

Dressing

Combine mayonnaise, sour cream, horseradish, salt, and celery seed. Set aside.

Assembly

Assemble salad by thinly layering potatoes, dressing, and parsley-onion mixture. Repeat layers in that order ending with the parsley-onion mixture. Do not stir! Cover and refrigerate at least 12 hours before serving.

SERVES 8 TO 10

Secret: This salad is best made the day before.

Lobster Salad

Salad

2 cups cooked and shredded lobster	¼ cup diced yellow pepper
¼ cup diced celery	½ cup seeded and diced tomato
1 teaspoon minced onion	Pinch salt

Dressing

1 tablespoon minced onion	½ tablespoon Dijon mustard
1 hard-boiled egg, chopped	1 tablespoon Worcestershire sauce
1 tablespoon capers	2 cups mayonnaise
½ tablespoon caper juice	Juice of 1 lemon
1 tablespoon diced dill gherkins	Juice of 1 lime
½ tablespoon dill gherkin juice	Bibb lettuce leaves

Salad

In a medium-sized bowl mix together lobster, celery, onion, yellow pepper, and tomato. Add a pinch of salt. Cover and refrigerate until chilled thoroughly.

Dressing

Combine onion, egg, capers, caper juice, pickles, pickle juice, mustard, Worcestershire sauce, mayonnaise, lemon juice, and lime juice in a food processor fitted with a steel blade. Process until thoroughly mixed.

Assembly

Drain lobster and add dressing until it reaches a good consistency. Serve on Bibb lettuce leaves.

SERVES 4

• •

Secret: If making salad for a large crowd, use
half shredded lobster and half cooked chopped shrimp.

• •

Marinated Cucumbers

3½ cups sliced cucumbers	1 cup sugar
2 onions, sliced	½ cup white vinegar
1 tablespoon salt	3 tablespoons water

Place cucumbers, onions and salt in a glass bowl. Place sugar, vinegar, and water in a saucepan and cook over medium heat until sugar dissolves. Cool mixture and pour over cucumbers. Cover and refrigerate for 48 hours.

SERVES 6

Paella Salad

This is an easy supper for the family or it can be doubled for a party or potluck gathering.
It's great to take to someone in need. Just add some crusty Cuban bread and flan for dessert.

1 (7-ounce) package yellow rice
2 tablespoons tarragon vinegar
⅓ cup oil
⅛ teaspoon salt
⅛ teaspoon dry mustard
2 cups diced cooked chicken

1 cup boiled shrimp, peeled and deveined
   (may omit)
1 large tomato, chopped
1 green bell pepper, chopped
½ cup minced onion
1 tablespoon chopped pimento
⅓ cup thinly sliced celery

Cook yellow rice according to package directions. Transfer rice to a large bowl and cool to room temperature.

In a small bowl mix together vinegar, oil, salt, and mustard. Pour vinegar and oil mixture over cooled rice and mix together well.

Add chicken, shrimp, tomato, green pepper, onion, pimento, and celery to rice. Cover and refrigerate until ready to serve.

SERVES 8

Secret: This is better made a day ahead.

Balsamic Garlic Vinaigrette

This salad dressing is so good, people have been known to dip their bread in it.

¼ cup balsamic vinegar
2 tablespoons granulated sugar
1 tablespoon minced garlic
2 tablespoons chopped fresh cilantro
   (optional)

⅛ teaspoon salt
¼ teaspoon white pepper
½ cup olive oil

Using a whisk, combine the vinegar, sugar, garlic, cilantro, salt, and pepper. Add the oil in a thin stream, blending until combined. Store in an airtight container in the refrigerator.

MAKES ¾ CUP

Secret: This recipe doubles well and keeps for a week or more in the refrigerator.

137

Blueberry-Buttermilk Coffee Cake

This is a great breakfast treat for house guests. It can be made ahead and freezes beautifully.

3 cups all-purpose flour
1 tablespoon baking powder
1 teaspoon salt
1⅔ cups sugar
¾ cup (1½ sticks) unsalted butter, room temperature

3 large eggs
1 tablespoon grated orange peel
2 teaspoons vanilla
¾ cup buttermilk
2 cups fresh blueberries, frozen
 Powdered sugar (optional)

Preheat oven to 350 degrees.

Butter and flour a 10-inch Bundt pan. Whisk flour, baking powder, and salt in a medium bowl. Using an electric mixer, beat sugar and butter in a large bowl until light and fluffy. Beat in eggs, 1 at a time. Beat in orange peel and vanilla. Beat in dry ingredients in 3 additions alternately with buttermilk in 2 additions. Fold in blueberries.

Pour batter into prepared pan. Bake about 1 hour or until a tester inserted near the center of cake comes out clean. Cool cake in pan on a baking rack 10 minutes. Turn cake out onto a rack and cool completely. Transfer cake to a plate, sift powdered sugar over, and serve.

SERVES 12

• •

Secret: Using frozen blueberries in the batter will keep the fruit from sinking to the bottom of the pan as the cake bakes. Place fresh berries in a single layer on a dinner plate, and put in freezer until frozen. (This does not take long.)

• •

Sour Cream Waffles

3 eggs, separated
⅔ cup milk
⅔ cup sour cream
1 teaspoon vanilla
½ cup (1 stick) butter, melted

1½ cups flour
1 tablespoon sugar
2 teaspoons baking powder
½ teaspoon baking soda
½ teaspoon salt

In a medium bowl, using an electric mixer, beat egg whites until stiff. Set aside.

In another medium bowl, beat egg yolks. Add milk, sour cream, vanilla, and butter to egg yolks. Beat until well mixed.

Sift together flour, sugar, baking powder, baking soda, and salt. Add flour mixture to egg mixture and beat. Fold egg whites into batter and let stand for at least 30 minutes before cooking.

Spoon batter onto warm waffle iron and cook until golden brown.

MAKES ABOUT 6 WAFFLES

Beef Stew On The Run

This is a great family meal for busy days. Just add a green salad and crusty bread.

2 pounds beef stew meat, raw	1 teaspoon salt
1 cup sliced carrots	Dash pepper
1 large potato, peeled and chopped into cubes	1 can tomato soup
	½ cup water
2 small onions, chopped	2 bay leaves

Preheat oven to 275 degrees.

Combine beef, carrots, potato, onions, salt, and pepper in a casserole. In a small bowl, mix together tomato soup and water, blending well. Pour over meat and vegetables. Cover and bake for 5 hours.

SERVES 6

Chicken Pot Pie

You can buy a cooked chicken and frozen puff pastry for this dish.
Both make this pot pie a very easy family meal or a meal to take to someone in need.

1 tablespoon olive oil	2½ cups chicken broth
1 tablespoon butter	½ (10-ounce) package frozen baby peas
1 large onion, chopped	¼ cup chopped fresh dill
2 teaspoons finely minced garlic	1 medium-sized ripe tomato, seeded and cut into ½ pieces
2 tablespoons all-purpose flour	
2 teaspoons dried tarragon	2½ cups chopped cooked chicken
3 carrots, halved and cut into 1-inch pieces (1½ cups)	Salt and pepper, to taste
	1 sheet (½-pound) puff pastry, thawed if frozen
1 Idaho potato, peeled and cut into ½-inch pieces (1 cup)	
1 green apple (Granny Smith), cored and cut into ½-inch pieces	1 egg mixed with 1 tablespoon water

Preheat oven to 350 degrees.

Heat oil and butter in a pot over low heat. Add onion and cook, stirring, for about 10 minutes. Add garlic and cook 2 minutes more. Sprinkle flour and tarragon over mixture and cook, stirring constantly, for 1 to 2 minutes more. Add carrots, potatoes, apple, and broth. Bring to a boil, reduce heat to a gentle simmer and cook, partially covered about 20 minutes or until the vegetables are tender. Add peas, dill, tomato, and chicken. Season to taste with salt and pepper and cook 5 minutes more. Spoon mixture into a 2-quart round casserole dish.

On a lightly floured surface, roll puff pastry out to form a circle 2-inches larger than the casserole. Brush some egg wash around the inside and outside of the casserole. Lay pastry over top, trim overhang to 1-inch, and crimp edges around rim to seal. Cut several slits in the pastry to release steam, then brush with remaining egg wash. Bake until crust is golden, about 40 to 45 minutes.

SERVES 6 TO 8

Bottega Spaghetti Pie

With its unique spaghetti crust, this makes a great family dinner.
Just add your favorite salad and you have a delicious meal.

Shell

½ (16-ounce) box thin spaghetti
⅓ cup grated Romano cheese
2 eggs, beaten

2 tablespoons butter
1 (15-ounce) package Ricotta cheese

Filling

½ pound ground chuck
½ pound mild Italian sausage
¼ cup chopped green pepper
½ cup chopped onion
1 (8-ounce) can tomato sauce

1 (4-ounce) can tomato paste
½ teaspoon garlic salt
½ teaspoon oregano
1 (4-ounce) package grated mozzarella cheese

Shell

Preheat oven to 350 degrees.

Cook spaghetti according to package directions. Drain, add grated Romano cheese, butter, and beaten eggs and mix well. Put mixture into a 9-inch pie plate to make a "crust". Spread the ricotta over the top of the spaghetti. Set aside.

Filling and Assembly

In a large skillet brown ground chuck, Italian sausage (squeeze sausage out of casing before browning), green pepper, and onion. Drain meat mixture and add tomato sauce, tomato paste, garlic salt, and oregano. Simmer until heated through.

Spoon meat mixture over ricotta and spaghetti crust. Bake in oven for 20 minutes. Sprinkle pie with mozzarella cheese. Heat about 5 minutes more or until cheese is melted. Cut into pie shaped wedges and serve.

SERVES 6 TO 8

• •
Secret: This can be frozen.
• •

Favorite Spaghetti Sauce

*During a bridge game the discussion turned to spaghetti sauce and one
Silver Sister's recipe. It got "best ever" reviews. We knew it had to be a "Rave Fave".*

2 tablespoons chopped garlic	2 tablespoons dried basil
1 cup chopped onions	¼ teaspoon dried oregano
¼ cup extra virgin olive oil	2 tablespoons ground black pepper
3 (28-ounce) cans tomato sauce	½ teaspoon salt
1 (12-ounce) can tomato paste	1 pound Italian sweet sausage links
1 cup water	2 pounds lean ground beef
¾ cup granulated sugar	

In a large stock pot, cook garlic and onions in olive oil over medium heat until golden brown. Add tomato sauce, tomato paste, and water. Add sugar, basil, oregano, black pepper and salt to tomato mixture. Cook over low heat for 1½ hours.

While sauce is cooking, remove casing from sausage and brown over medium heat in a large skillet. Add ground beef and brown. Drain off the fat. Add the meat mixture to the tomato sauce. The sauce is best if made the day before serving.

SERVES 10 TO12

Secret: This makes a lot and can be put into smaller portions for freezing.

Fireside Casserole

*This is a favorite casserole for church suppers. Volunteers are asked to make
a casserole and bring it to the church hot. To make the casseroles more uniform, each volunteer
is given a disposable pan to make it in, a package of noodles, and the recipe.*

1 (8-ounce) package medium egg noodles	1 (8-ounce) package cream cheese
1 tablespoon butter	½ cup sour cream
1 pound ground beef chuck	⅓ cup minced green onions
2 (8-ounce) cans tomato paste	1 tablespoon minced green pepper
½ pound (8-ounces) cottage cheese	1 tablespoon butter, melted

Cook noodles according to package directions. Drain and set aside.

Melt butter in a medium skillet and sauté beef in tomato paste. Remove from heat and set aside.

In a medium bowl combine cottage cheese, cream cheese, sour cream, green onions, and green pepper. Place half the noodles in a 2-quart casserole and cover with cheese mixture. Cover with remainder of the noodles. Pour melted butter over noodles, then tomato-meat sauce. Cover and refrigerate for several hours or overnight. Bake covered for about 45 minutes.

SERVES 6 TO 8

Grouper LaFitte

This dish makes good fish extraordinary! Everyone will think you spent hours in the kitchen, but 30 minutes will do it. Adding the shrimp is an easy upgrade.

2   large eggs
1   cup milk
2   cups all-purpose flour
1½ teaspoons Creole seasoning, divided
4   grouper fillets (about 1½-pounds)
    Vegetable oil
12 large fresh shrimp, peeled and deveined
1   tablespoon butter

2   teaspoons minced garlic
¼   cup vermouth
2   cups whipping cream
¼   cup chopped green onions, divided
2   teaspoons lemon juice
3   very thin slices cooked ham, cut into
    strips
    Lemon slices, for garnish

Whisk together eggs and milk in a shallow dish. Combine flour and 1 teaspoon Creole seasoning in another shallow dish. Dredge fillets in flour mixture, dip in egg mixture, and dredge in flour again.

Pour oil (about 3-inches deep) into a heavy large skillet and heat to 360 degrees. Fry grouper fillets 6 minutes or until golden brown. Drain on clean brown paper bags (fish will not stick to bags). Keep fish warm in the oven set on warm.

Melt butter in a heavy large skillet over medium heat. Add shrimp and minced garlic and cook, stirring often until shrimp turn pink. Remove shrimp and reserve drippings left in skillet. Stir vermouth into reserved drippings, bring mixture to a boil, and cook 1 minute. Add whipping cream, 2 tablespoons green onions, lemon juice, and ½ teaspoon Creole seasoning. Cook, stirring often, about 12 to 15 minutes or until mixture thickens.

To serve, place grouper fillets on a serving platter, drizzle with sauce. Top with shrimp and ham and sprinkle with remaining green onions. Garnish with lemon slices, if desired.

SERVES 6

Grouper on the Grill with Vegetables

This recipe was invented in a moment of desperation. A Silver Sister was having a casual dinner party and a few more people were added to the guest list. To make the grouper go further, lots of veggies were added. Now friends and family beg for this delicious classic.

Vegetables

¼ cup (½ stick) butter (or more if needed)
1 red pepper, chopped
1 green pepper, chopped
1 yellow pepper, chopped

1 large sweet onion, chopped
1 pint grape or cherry tomatoes, cut in half
Seasoned salt (Jane's Krazy Mixed-Up Salt)

Grouper

2 pounds fresh grouper fillet
Olive oil
Seasoned salt (Jane's Krazy Mixed-Up Salt)

Powdered garlic
Freshly ground black pepper
4 Fresh lemons, cut in half

Vegetables

Prepare the grill.

Put butter, red peppers, green peppers, yellow peppers, and onions on a double thickness heavy duty piece of foil with the edges folded up, tray style. Sprinkle with lots of Jane's salt. Place vegetable filled foil tray on the grill. Sauté the vegetables until tender, adding the tomatoes when the other veggies are almost done. Continue cooking until the tomatoes are warm throughout.

Grouper

Wash and dry grouper fillet. Coat fillet with olive oil. Sprinkle seasoned salt, garlic, ground black pepper, and lemon juice over the top. Make another foil tray for grouper. Place prepared grouper on foil tray and grill over a medium fire until the flesh is firm. Put fillet on the grill just before adding the tomatoes to the vegetables. Transfer the grouper to a large platter and cover with the cooked vegetables.

SERVES 4 TO 6

Glorious Shrimp

3 pounds medium to large white shrimp, peeled and deveined	½ teaspoon sea salt or Krazy Jane's Mixed-Up Salt
½ pound (2 sticks) butter, melted	½ teaspoon cayenne pepper (optional)
2 cloves garlic, crushed	2 cups soft bread crumbs
½ teaspoon paprika	(8 to 10 slices white bread)
	⅓ cup chopped fresh parsley

Preheat oven to 350 degrees.

Rinse peeled and deveined shrimp, drain, and pat dry.

Mix together butter, garlic, paprika, salt, and cayenne pepper. Set the butter mixture aside.

Use the food processor fitted with the steel blade to make bread crumbs. Add parsley to bread crumbs and mix well. Toss shrimp and bread crumb mixture in a large bowl.

Arrange shrimp in a buttered 9 x 13-inch baking dish. Pour butter mixture over shrimp. Bake 20 to 30 minutes, or until bubbly. Stir half way through baking.

SERVES 8 TO 10

● ●

Secret: Use ½ cup olive oil and ½ cup (1 stick) butter in place of all butter.

● ●

Hot Chicken Salad with Water Chestnuts

This is great to serve to company with fresh fruit salad and crusty French bread.

¾ cup good mayonnaise	1 (8-ounce) can sliced water chestnuts, drained
1 tablespoon lemon juice	
¼ teaspoon celery salt	¼ cup sliced ripe olives
1 teaspoon seasoned salt (Essence of Emeril)	3 cups cut-up chicken (may use store bought rotisserie chicken)
1 (8-ounce) box fresh mushrooms, cooked in 1-2 tablespoons butter until golden brown	1 cup grated sharp Cheddar cheese

Preheat oven to 350 degrees.

Lightly grease a 9 x 13 x 2-inch casserole dish. Mix together mayonnaise, lemon juice, celery salt, seasoned salt, cooked mushrooms, water chestnuts, olives, and chicken. Transfer mixture to prepared casserole. Sprinkle Cheddar cheese over top and bake for 30 minutes or until bubbly.

SERVES 6 TO 8

144

Salmon in Saffron Mussel Sauce

The mussels and sauce are good enough to eat plain or over pasta.

Mussels

1 pound mussels, scrubbed and debearded	½ cup dry white wine ½ teaspoon saffron threads, crushed

Sauce

¾ cup whipping cream	1 garlic clove, minced
½ cup canned crushed tomatoes with added purée	1 bay leaf
	⅛ teaspoon cayenne pepper

Salmon

1 tablespoon olive oil	4 (8-ounce) skinless salmon fillets

Mussels

Combine mussels and wine in large saucepan over medium high heat. Cover and cook until mussels begin to open, stirring occasionally, about 4 minutes. Using slotted spoon, transfer mussels to large bowl (discard any mussels that do not open). Pour liquid from saucepan into 2 cup measuring cup. Stir in saffron. Let cooking liquid stand 15 minutes.

Sauce

Add enough cream to cooking liquid to measure 1⅓ cups. Transfer to large saucepan. Stir in tomatoes, garlic, bay leaf, and cayenne. Simmer over medium heat until sauce thickens slightly, about 5 minutes. Season with salt and pepper. (Can be made 4 hours ahead. Cover and refrigerate mussels and sauce separately.)

Salmon

Heat oil in large nonstick skillet over high heat. Add salmon, rounded side down. Cook until bottom is golden, about 3 minutes. Turn salmon over. Reduce heat to low. Cover and cook until salmon is opaque in center, about 4 minutes longer. Remove from heat. Leave covered to keep warm.

Assembly

Remove mussels and sauce from the refrigerator. Bring sauce in large saucepan to simmer over low heat. Add mussels. Stir until heated through, about 2 minutes. Place 1 salmon fillet on each of 4 plates. Divide mussels among plates. Spoon sauce over salmon and mussels.

SERVES 4

• •

Secret: This is great served on a large platter over saffron risotto.

• •

Short Ribs Provençal

You can prepare these well in advance and reheat them before dinner.

2   tablespoons olive oil
6   pounds meaty beef short ribs
    Salt
    Freshly ground black pepper
1   large onion, finely chopped
1   medium carrot, finely chopped
1   celery stalk, finely chopped
12 whole garlic cloves, peeled
2   tablespoons all-purpose flour

1   tablespoon dried Herbes de Provence
2   cups red Zinfandel
2½ cups canned beef broth
1   (14-ounce) can diced tomatoes in juice
1   bay leaf
½   cup (about) water
24 baby carrots, peeled
½   cup Niçoise olives
3   tablespoons chopped fresh parsley

Preheat oven to 325 degrees.

Heat 2 tablespoons oil in heavy large ovenproof pot over medium-high heat. Sprinkle ribs with salt and pepper. Working in batches, add ribs to pot and brown well, turning often, about 8 minutes per batch. Using tongs, transfer ribs to large bowl.

Pour off all but 2 tablespoons drippings from pot or add oil as necessary to measure 2 tablespoons. Add onion, carrot, and celery and cook over medium low heat until vegetables are soft, stirring frequently, about 10 minutes. Add garlic, flour, and Herbes de Provence. Stir vegetables for one minute. Add wine and 2 cups broth. Bring to a boil over high heat, scraping up browned bits. Add tomatoes with juices and bay leaf.

Return ribs and any accumulated juices to pot. If necessary, add enough water to pot to barely cover ribs. Bring to a boil. Cover pot tightly and transfer to oven. Bake until ribs are very tender, stirring occasionally, about 2 hours and 15 minutes. (Can be made one day ahead. Cool slightly, then refrigerate uncovered until cold. Cover and keep refrigerated.)

When ready to continue bring ribs to a simmer. Add remaining ½ cup broth, peeled baby carrots and Niçoise olives to pot. Press carrots gently to submerge. Cover, return to oven, and continue cooking at 350 degrees until carrots are tender, about 15 minutes. Discard bay leaf.

Transfer short ribs and carrots to a platter. Tent with foil to keep warm. If necessary, boil sauce to thicken slightly. Season to taste with salt and pepper. Pour sauce over short ribs. Sprinkle with parsley.

SERVES 6

Slow Cooker Barbecued Pork Sandwiches

These little sandwiches are easy to prepare and make great appetizers for a casual party.

1 (3-pound) boneless pork loin roast, trimmed	1-2 tablespoons hot sauce
1 cup water	1 teaspoon salt
1 (18-ounce) bottle barbecue sauce	1 teaspoon pepper
¼ cup (packed) brown sugar	24 miniature rolls (special order at bakery)
2 tablespoons Worcestershire sauce	Coleslaw (store bought)

Place pork roast in a 4-quart slow cooker and add water. Cover and cook on high 7 hours or until meat is tender.

When tender, stir meat with a fork to shred. Add barbecue sauce, brown sugar, Worcestershire sauce, hot sauce, salt, and pepper to pork and mix well.

Reduce setting to low and cook, covered for 1 hour. Serve barbecue on miniature rolls with a dollop of coleslaw.

24 SANDWICHES

Corn Pie with Roasted Red Peppers and Green Chiles

1 (7-ounce) jar roasted red bell peppers, drained	2 teaspoons salt
2 (10-ounce) packages frozen corn, thawed	1 cup sour cream (nonfat may be used)
	1 cup (4-ounces) grated Swiss cheese
1 cup (2 sticks) butter, melted	1 cup (4-ounces) grated extra sharp Cheddar cheese
4 eggs, beaten	1 (4-ounce) can chopped green chiles
1 cup yellow cornmeal	

Preheat oven to 350 degrees.

Rinse bell peppers and pat dry with paper towels. Chop bell peppers. Blend corn in a blender at low speed until partially puréed but not smooth. Pour into a large bowl. Add butter, eggs, cornmeal, salt, sour cream, Swiss cheese, Cheddar cheese, bell peppers, and green chiles and mix well. Pour into a greased 10-inch deep-dish pie plate (do not overfill). Bake for 40 to 45 minutes or until golden brown and firm to the touch.

SERVES 8

Secret: You may double the recipe using three (9-inch) pie plates.

Tuscan Chicken Cakes
with Tomato-Basil Relish

This is an impressive and easy dish to make for a ladies' luncheon.
Use any leftover Tomato-Basil Relish for an hors d'oeuvre served with Pita Crisps.

Golden Aïoli

½ cup mayonnaise

2 tablespoons honey mustard

Tomato-Basil Relish

1 cup seeded, chopped plum tomatoes
⅓ cup chopped red onion
3 tablespoons drained, chopped sun-dried
   tomatoes

2 tablespoons slivered fresh basil leaves
2 tablespoons purchased balsamic vinegar
   and oil dressing
2 tablespoons purchased basil pesto

Chicken Cakes

3 cups cooked chicken, shredded and
   chopped (to make it easy use a
   purchased rotisserie chicken)
1 cup Italian seasoned bread crumbs,
   divided
¼ cup mayonnaise
1 egg, slightly beaten

¼ cup purchased basil pesto
2 tablespoons honey mustard
⅓ cup finely chopped red onion
2 tablespoons olive oil
1 (5-ounce) package mixed salad greens
⅓ cup purchased balsamic vinegar and oil
   dressing

Golden Aïoli

In a small bowl, whisk together mayonnaise and mustard. Set aside

Tomato-Basil Relish

In a small bowl, mix together plum tomatoes, onion, sun-dried tomatoes, basil leaves, balsamic dressing, and basil pesto. Set aside.

Chicken Cakes

In a large bowl, mix together chicken, ½ cup bread crumbs, mayonnaise, egg, pesto, mustard, and onion. Using a ⅓ cup measure, shape chicken mixture into 8 cakes. Lightly coat each cake, using remaining ½ cup bread crumbs.

Place oil in a nonstick skillet over medium-high heat. Add chicken cakes and cook until golden brown, about 3 minutes per side. Drain on paper towels.

Toss mixed greens with balsamic dressing and divide among 4 serving plates. Top each plate of greens with 2 chicken cakes. Drizzle with golden aïoli and top with a dollop of Tomato-Basil Relish.

SERVES 4

148

Butternut Squash Gratin

This is a great side dish to serve in the Fall when squash are plentiful.

Squash

¼ cup (½ stick) unsalted butter
4 cups thinly sliced onions (about 1 pound)
2½ pounds butternut squash, peeled,
    seeded, cut into ½-inch cubes

1 teaspoon sugar
½ teaspoon salt
½ teaspoon ground black pepper
¾ cup canned low-salt chicken broth

Topping

2 cups fresh bread crumbs (made from
    8 slices soft white bread)
2 cups (packed) grated sharp white
    Cheddar cheese

1½ tablespoons chopped fresh rosemary
½ teaspoon dried thyme

Squash and Topping

Preheat oven to 350 degrees.

Butter 13 x 9 x 2-inch glass baking dish. Melt butter in heavy large skillet over medium-high heat. Add onions, cook until light golden, about 8 minutes. Add squash and cook 4 minutes. Sprinkle sugar, salt, and pepper over vegetables and continue cooking until onions and squash begin to caramelize, about 5 minutes.

Spread vegetable mixture in prepared dish. Pour chicken broth over vegetables. Cover tightly with foil and bake 45 minutes. (Squash mixture can be made 1 day ahead. Cool, then cover and refrigerate. Reheat in 350 degree oven until heated through, about 10 minutes.)

Increase oven temperature to 400 degrees. Mix bread crumbs, cheese, rosemary, and thyme in medium bowl. Sprinkle over gratin. Bake uncovered about 30 minutes or until top is golden brown and crisp.

SERVES 10

Fourth of July Baked Beans

These beans are yummy and easy to make.
Men love them. They are great for picnics or with burgers.

3 (1 pound) packages hot pork sausage	1 cup prepared yellow mustard
3 (18-ounce) cans baked beans (B&M)	1 (1 pound) box dark brown sugar
1 large (32-ounce) bottle ketchup (Hunts)	1 large onion, chopped

Preheat oven to 300 degrees.

Break sausage into bite-size pieces and place in a large baking pan and bake. Drain grease off and pat sausage with paper towels to absorb grease. Add beans, ketchup, mustard, brown sugar and onion. Mix together until well blended. Pour bean mixture into two 13 x 9-inch casseroles and bake for 2½ hours. Remove from oven and let casserole stand for 10 minutes before serving.

SERVES 20 TO 24

• •

Secret: This seems like a lot of sausage and ketchup but these ingredients are key to these decadent, meaty beans. Do not skimp on anything.

• •

Green Bean Bundles

If a vegetable can be adorable this is it. It's easy to prepare and looks like you've worked hard.

5 slices bacon	4 tablespoons brown sugar
1 pound fresh green beans	1 teaspoon Worcestershire sauce
4 tablespoons unsalted butter	

Preheat oven to 375 degrees.

Line a 9 x 13-inch baking pan with foil. Cook bacon in a heavy skillet over medium-low heat until partially done. Drain on paper towels, then cut each slice in half and set aside.

Bring a large saucepan of water to a boil over high heat. Add green beans, cook 2 minutes, drain and rinse under cold water. Set aside.

Melt butter in a small saucepan over medium-low heat. Add sugar, soy sauce, and Worcestershire and cook 1 minute, stirring until sugar is dissolved. Remove from heat.

Take a small bundle (7 to 8 beans) and wrap with a bacon half. Place in baking pan. Repeat with remaining beans and bacon. Use a pastry brush to coat bundles with butter mixture. Bake 20 minutes or until bacon is done. The bacon should be cooked through, and the beans should retain their bright color.

MAKES 10 BUNDLES

Fried Fresh Corn

This corn is a great summer treat.

12   ears fresh corn
8   slices bacon, uncooked
½   cup butter

2-4 tablespoons sugar
2   teaspoons salt
½   teaspoon fresh ground pepper

Cut off tips of corn kernels into a large bowl. Scrape milk and remaining pulp from cob with a paring knife. Set aside.

Cook bacon in a large skillet until crisp. Remove bacon and drain on paper towels. Reserve about ¼ cup drippings in skillet. Crumble bacon and set aside.

Add corn, butter, sugar, salt, and pepper to drippings in skillet. Cook over medium heat 20 minutes, stirring frequently. Spoon corn into a serving dish and sprinkle with crumbled bacon.

SERVES 12

Roasted Cauliflower
with Caper and Olive Sauce

Roasted Cauliflower

1   large head cauliflower, cut into small
     florets
2-3 tablespoons olive oil

Kosher salt
Freshly ground black pepper

Caper and Olive Sauce

⅓   cup olive oil
2   teaspoons minced garlic
4   tablespoons capers, drained

¼   cup Kalamata olives
Fresh squeezed lemon juice

Roasted Cauliflower

Preheat oven to 400 degrees.

Place cauliflower in a large zip-top plastic bag and add oil. Shake gently to cover. Add salt and pepper and shake again. Arrange cauliflower on a heavy baking sheet and roast until lightly browned and tender, about 20 to 25 minutes, rotating sheet halfway through.

Caper and Olive Sauce

In a small saucepan, combine olive oil, garlic, capers, and olives. Warm over low heat for 5 minutes. Pour over roasted cauliflower, and toss to coat. Just before serving, squeeze fresh lemon juice over top of cauliflower.

SERVES 4 TO 6

Roasted Green Beans

These beans are low-fat and delicious.

1¼ pounds green beans, trimmed	½ teaspoon kosher salt
2 tablespoons slivered almonds	¼ teaspoon garlic powder
1 tablespoon lemon juice	¼ teaspoon dried basil
2 teaspoons olive oil	¼ teaspoon ground black pepper

Preheat oven to 450 degrees.

Combine green beans, almonds, lemon juice, oil, salt, garlic powder, basil, and pepper in a jelly-roll pan, tossing well. Bake for 10 minutes or until beans are tender and browned, stirring often. Serve immediately.

SERVES 4

Spinach Pie Topped with Phyllo Strips

This Greek-style dish is a great make ahead item.
When you are ready to bake, it can go straight from the freezer into the oven.

½ cup plus 2 tablespoons olive oil	½ cup grated Parmesan cheese
4 medium onions, chopped	2 teaspoons dried dill
6 garlic cloves, minced	½ teaspoon nutmeg
4 teaspoons kosher salt, divided	½ teaspoon ground black pepper
6 (10-ounce) packages spinach, thawed and squeezed dry	8 large eggs, lightly beaten
1 pound feta cheese, crumbled	8 ounces (½ package) frozen phyllo sheets, thawed and thinly sliced

Preheat oven to 375 degrees.

In a large nonstick skillet, heat 2 tablespoons oil over medium-high heat. Add onions, cook, stirring occasionally, until translucent, 3 to 5 minutes. Add garlic and 2 teaspoons salt. Cook until garlic is tender, about 1 to 2 minutes.

Transfer mixture to a large bowl. Stir in spinach, feta, Parmesan, dill, nutmeg, pepper, and remaining 2 teaspoons salt. Fold eggs into spinach mixture until combined. Divide mixture between 2 (9-inch) springform pans. Press firmly to flatten.

In a large bowl, gently toss sliced phyllo to separate, then toss with remaining ½ cup oil until coated. Cover tops of each pie evenly with phyllo strips. Bake until heated through and topping is golden brown, about 30 minutes.

SERVES 12 TO 14

● ●

Secret: Pies may be frozen for up to 3 months. To freeze, cover pies tightly with plastic wrap, being careful not to flatten topping. Do not thaw before baking. Bake frozen pie at 375 degrees for about 1 hour and 15 minutes.

● ●

Sweet Potato Brûlée

*This is a different twist on sweet potatoes and great served with
Thanksgiving dinner. To make things easy, it can be made 2 days ahead.*

Sweet Potatoes

2   large red-skinned sweet potatoes (about 3 pounds) or 3 (1 pound) cans sweet potatoes

Custard

¾ cup whipping cream
3   large egg yolks
1½ tablespoons (packed) golden brown sugar
1   teaspoon salt

½ teaspoon coarsely ground black pepper
¼ teaspoon ground cinnamon
⅛ teaspoon ground nutmeg
4   tablespoons sugar

Sweet Potatoes

Preheat oven to 375 degrees.

Pierce sweet potatoes and place on oven rack. Bake until tender, about 1 hour. Cool 30 minutes and peel. Place in food processor fitted with the steel blade, and mix until smooth.

Custard

Whisk cream, egg yolks, brown sugar, salt, pepper, cinnamon, and nutmeg in a large bowl to blend. Whisk 2½ cups potato purée into cream mixture (reserve remaining purée for another use).

Assembly

Preheat oven to 350 degrees.

Butter a 4 to 6 cup soufflé dish. Pour sweet potato custard into prepared dish. Place dish in 13 x 9 x 2-inch metal baking pan. Add enough hot water to pan to come halfway up side of soufflé dish. Cover pan with foil. Bake custard 1 hour. Uncover pan and bake custard until firm in center, about 15 minutes. Remove from water, refrigerate uncovered until cold, at least 2 hours. (Can be made 2 days ahead. Cover tightly and refrigerate.)

Preheat oven to 350 degrees. Transfer custard to baking sheet. Rewarm, uncovered, in oven for 15 minutes.

Preheat broiler. Sprinkle ½ tablespoon sugar over custard. Broil custard until sugar topping melts and browns, rotating sheet to broil evenly, about 2 minutes. Serve warm.

8 SERVINGS

• •

Secret: This recipe was tested using fresh sweet potatoes and canned sweet potatoes.
There was no difference in the taste of the dish. Make life easy and used canned sweet potatoes.

• •

Orzo with Portobello Mushrooms

1 pound (16-ounces) orzo
5 quarts chicken broth
½ pound Portobello mushrooms, roughly
   chopped
½ pound white mushrooms, roughly
   chopped

4 tablespoons extra virgin olive oil
2 cups dry white wine
1 (10-ounce) bag baby spinach
1 cup grated Parmesan cheese
2 teaspoons kosher salt
2 teaspoons freshly ground black pepper

In a large stockpot, cook orzo in chicken broth for 15 to 20 minutes and drain.

In a large skillet, cook mushrooms in olive oil over medium-high heat for 5 minutes. Add wine and spinach and cook for 1 minute. Remove skillet from heat and stir in orzo and Parmesan. Season with salt and pepper.

SERVE 8 TO 12

Fresh Cranberry Relish

A great accompaniment for poultry or pork.

2 (12-ounce) bags whole cranberries
2 tart red apples, quartered and cored
2-3 oranges (thin-skinned), quartered and
   seeded

1½-2 cups finely chopped pecans
1 cup sugar

Prepare at least 24 hours in advance. In a food grinder or a food processor fitted with the steel blade, finely chop cranberries, apples, and oranges. (Do not peel the apples or oranges and chop each fruit separately.) Combine the ground fruit and its juice with the chopped pecans and sugar until well mixed. Place in an airtight container and refrigerate. This will keep for 2 weeks in the refrigerator. May be frozen.

MAKES ABOUT 6 CUPS

Marvelous Marinade

*This marinade tastes great on all kinds of meat. Use it on
chicken, pork, hamburgers, and steaks. No refrigerator should be without it!*

1 cup oil (may be omitted)
1 (10-ounce) bottle soy sauce
½ cup lemon juice

1 (6-ounce) bottle Worcestershire sauce
2 cloves garlic, minced
1 small jar prepared mustard

Combine oil, soy sauce, lemon juice, Worcestershire sauce, garlic, and mustard in a large covered container and shake well to dissolve. This marinade will keep in the refrigerator for weeks.

MAKES 4 CUPS

Hot Mustard

This tangy mustard adds a new dimension to sandwiches, especially ham. It also makes a coveted Christmas gift for friends. Just put mustard in cute jars and tie with a ribbon.

2	regular cans dry mustard (Coleman)	3	eggs, beaten
1	cup malt vinegar	1	cup sugar

Combine mustard and vinegar, soak overnight. Add eggs and sugar to mustard mixture. Cook in double boiler over simmering water, beating constantly until thickened, about 10 to 20 minutes. This doubles easily.

MAKES 2 CUPS

• •

Secret: For the Special Occasion Reception double recipe.

• •

Repickled Pickles

2	quarts kosher dill pickles and garlic	1	teaspoon mustard seed
3	cups sugar	1	teaspoon celery seed
1	cup vinegar	15	cloves

Drain pickles and garlic, slice into rounds and place in a covered mixing bowl. In a medium bowl mix together sugar, vinegar, mustard seed, celery seed, and cloves. Pour over sliced pickles and garlic. Let stand 24 hours, stirring occasionally. Put pickle mixture in a clear covered jar and refrigerate.

MAKES 2 QUARTS

Pots de Crème

This recipe is an old one. It is delightful served in demi-tasse cups with a candied violet on top.

1 (4-ounce) German sweet chocolate bar
    (Baker's)
1½ cups light cream
¼ cup sugar

6 egg yolks, slightly beaten
1 teaspoon vanilla
    Candied violets or whipped cream, for
    garnish

Use a double boiler to melt chocolate and cream over hot water. Blend in sugar until satin-smooth. Slightly beat egg yolks. Gradually stir yolks into hot chocolate mixture and cook, stirring constantly, 7 minutes or until mixture is like thin pudding. Stir in vanilla. Pour into small cups. (Mixture thickens as it stands.) Refrigerate until ready to serve. Serve topped with either a candied violet, a dollop of whipped cream or both.

SERVES 4 TO 5

𝒜 Silver Sister received this recipe one Christmas from her husband's aunt. It came with a lovely set of demi-tasse cups that belonged to the aunt, and a box of candied violets. The aunt loved to entertain and wrote this message with the gift: "I have served this recipe for years. It is foolproof and far superior, in my notion, to any of those more modern versions of a chocolate mousse. It is a darker and richer version (no egg whites). I have served it in the demi-tasse cups with a violet atop to raves from all guests – particularly men. To see them address themselves to this tiny elegant dessert with tiny spoons is an experience, I can tell you! They love it! And are so careful!"

Cream Cheese Pound Cake

This very moist cake is delicious all by itself for a snack. For a special dessert serve it with fresh berries and whipped cream or ice cream and chocolate sauce.

1½ cups unsalted butter, room temperature
1 (8-ounce) package cream cheese, room temperature
3 cups sugar

6 large eggs
1½ teaspoons vanilla
2 cups all-purpose flour
⅛ teaspoon salt

Preheat oven to 300 degrees.

Grease and flour a 10-inch tube pan. Using an electric mixer, beat butter and cream cheese in a medium bowl at medium speed for 2 minutes. Gradually add sugar and beat for 5 minutes or until light and fluffy. Add eggs, one at a time, beating just until the yellow disappears. Add vanilla and mix well.

Sift together flour and salt. Gradually add flour to butter mixture, beating at low speed, after each addition, just until blended. Transfer batter to prepared tube pan and bake 1 hour 30 minutes or until a wooden toothpick inserted near the center comes out clean. When cake is done, cool on a wire rack for 10 to 15 minutes. Remove from pan and cool completely.

SERVES 12 TO 15

● ●

Secret: To keep cake from drying out, fill an ovenproof measuring cup with 2 cups water and place in oven before baking cake. Leave cup in oven until cake is removed.

● ●

Fresh Apple Cake with Caramel Glaze

This is a decadently delicious gooey cake. Great for a morning meeting as well as a special dessert served with vanilla ice cream.

Cake

1½ cups vegetable oil	1 teaspoon vanilla
2 cups sugar	3 eggs, beaten
3 cups all-purpose flour	3 cups peeled, diced fresh tart apples
1 teaspoon salt	(about 4 apples)
1 teaspoon baking soda	1 cup chopped pecans or walnuts

Preheat oven to 350 degrees.

Do not use mixer. Sift together flour, sugar, salt, and soda. Add oil, eggs, and vanilla. Mix thoroughly. Batter will be very thick. Mix in apples and nuts. Pour batter into a slightly greased (do not flour) Bundt pan. Bake for 50 minutes or until a wooden toothpick inserted in the center comes out clean. Cool slightly and invert on a serving plate.

Glaze

½ cup (1 stick) butter	¼ cup milk
1 cup (packed) light brown sugar	

In a small saucepan combine butter, brown sugar, and milk. Cook over medium-high heat and bring mixture to a boil. Boil for 3 to 5 minutes. Pour hot glaze over warm cake. Let cake cool. Cover and store in the refrigerator. This is better after a day in the refrigerator. May be frozen.

SERVES 12 TO 15

Orange-Date Cake

This is a fabulous cake for the holidays. Even people who don't like dates love this cake.

Cake

1	cup butter	1	cup buttermilk
1¾	cups sugar	3	tablespoons orange juice
3	eggs	½	teaspoon vanilla
3	cups cake flour	½	teaspoon almond extract
1	teaspoon baking soda	1	tablespoon grated orange zest
½	teaspoon baking powder	1	cup chopped dates
1	teaspoon salt	1	cup chopped English walnuts

Icing

1	cup sugar	Whipped cream, for garnish	
1	cup orange juice	Orange zest, for garnish	
	Zest of 1 orange		

Cake

Preheat oven to 350 degrees.

Grease a 10-inch tube pan. Using an electric mixer, beat together butter and sugar in a large bowl until light and fluffy. Beat in eggs one at a time. Set batter aside.

In a medium bowl, sift together flour, baking soda, baking powder, and salt. In another bowl, combine buttermilk, orange juice, vanilla, and almond extract. Add flour and buttermilk mixtures alternately to batter, beginning and ending with flour. Add orange zest, dates, and walnuts and mix until well combined.

Transfer batter to the prepared tube pan and bake for 1 hour and 15 minutes or until a toothpick inserted near the center comes out clean.

Icing

Combine sugar and orange juice in a bowl and whisk until smooth. Add orange zest and mix until well blended. Pour icing over hot cake as soon as cake is removed from the oven. Allow cake to cool completely before removing from pan. Serve with whipped cream and garnish with orange zest if desired.

SERVES 12 TO 15

Secret: Wrap cake carefully in plastic wrap
and store in the refrigerator. It will keep well for days.

So-Easy-It's-Nutty Chocolate Cake

Cake

1 cup sugar	1 teaspoon baking powder
½ cup (1 stick) butter, softened	⅓ cup cocoa powder
1 unbeaten egg	½ teaspoon baking soda
1½ cups flour	½ cup boiling water
¼ teaspoon salt	

Topping

¾ cup brown sugar	½ cup (1 stick) butter, softened
¼ cup cream	1½ cups chopped pecans

Cake

Preheat oven to 350 degrees.

In a large bowl, put in sugar, butter, and unbeaten egg. On top of that sift flour, salt, baking powder, cocoa powder, and baking soda. On top of that pour boiling water. Using an electric mixer, beat ingredients for 3 minutes until smooth. Pour into a 9-inch square pan. Bake for 30 minutes.

Topping

While cake is baking, mix together brown sugar, cream, butter, and chopped nuts. Pour over hot baked cake and broil 8 to 10 inches from heat source for about 2 minutes or until browned.

MAKES 1 (9-INCH) CAKE

Holiday Nuggets

These melt-in-your mouth morsels are the best we have ever tasted.

½ cup shortening	2 cups flour
½ cup butter	½ teaspoon salt
½ cup powdered sugar	½ cup chopped walnuts
1 tablespoon vanilla	Powdered sugar
1 teaspoon almond extract	

Preheat oven to 325 degrees.

Beat together shortening, butter, and sugar in a large bowl using an electric mixer. Add vanilla and almond extract, beating until smooth and creamy.

Sift together flour and salt, and add to the butter mixture with the mixer on low speed until just combined. Gently mix in nuts.

Roll dough into 1 to 1½-inch balls and place on an ungreased cookie sheet. Bake for 15 minutes. Remove from cookie sheet and roll in powdered sugar.

MAKES 24 TO 30

Caramel-Walnut Pie with Dried Cherries

Not quite as sweet as a pecan pie, but with the same caramel candy-like filling.

1¼ cups dried tart cherries, chopped
½ cup Ruby Port
⅔ cup (packed) golden brown sugar
⅔ cup light corn syrup
3 large eggs
¼ cup (½ stick) butter, melted

1½ teaspoons vanilla
1 cup walnuts, toasted and chopped
Purchased 9-inch pie crust or your favorite homemade
Whipped cream, for garnish

Preheat oven to 350 degrees.

Boil cherries and Port in heavy small saucepan until Port is absorbed, stirring often, about 10 minutes. Cool completely.

Using an electric mixer, beat brown sugar, corn syrup, eggs, and melted butter in a large bowl until foamy. Beat in vanilla. Stir in walnuts and Port-infused cherries.

Pour filling into prepared crust and bake about 50 minutes or until crust is golden and filling is brown and just set in the center. Cool pie completely and serve with whipped cream.

SERVES 8 TO 10

Miniature Caramel-Walnut Tarts with Dried Cherries

1 (3-ounce) package cream cheese
½ cup butter
1 cup all-purpose flour

Preheat oven to 325 degrees. Soften cream cheese and butter.
Stir in flour and mix well. Wrap dough in plastic wrap and refrigerate 1 hour or longer. When well chilled, shape dough into 24 balls and press into miniature muffin pans. Shape dough with your fingers to look like tiny pie crusts.
Put 1 tablespoon of filling from Caramel-Walnut Pie with Dried Cherries into each crust. Bake for 20 to 30 minutes or until set.

MAKES 24

White Chocolate Raspberry Pie

This was a hit at one Silver Sister's parent's fiftieth wedding anniversary party.

1   (9-inch) pie shell, baked and cooled

Filling

2   (10-ounce) packages frozen raspberries
    in light syrup

4   tablespoons granulated sugar
2   tablespoons cornstarch

Butter Cream

6   ounces white chocolate
¾   cup (1½ sticks) unsalted butter
⅓   cup granulated sugar

¾   teaspoon vanilla
3   eggs, room temperature

Glaze

4   (1-ounce) squares bitter sweet chocolate   ¼   cup (½ stick) unsalted butter

Filling

In a food processor fitted with the steel blade, purée raspberries then strain. In a saucepan stir together sugar and cornstarch. Mix in raspberries, stirring until smooth. Cook stirring constantly until mixture comes to a full boil. Remove from heat and set the pan in ice water for 5 to 10 minutes. Cover filling and refrigerate.

Butter Cream

Melt white chocolate carefully and cool. Beat sugar and butter with an electric mixer for 2 to 3 minutes or until light and fluffy. Add white chocolate to butter mixture. Add eggs one at a time and beat until fluffy. Stir in vanilla.

Glaze

Melt bittersweet chocolate and butter together.

Assembly

Pour raspberry filling into pie shell then carefully layer butter cream filling over raspberries. Refrigerate for several hours. Before serving drizzle a very thin coat of chocolate glaze over chilled pie. (You will have chocolate left over.)

SERVES 8

• •

Secret: Do not make the bittersweet
chocolate layer too thick or the pie will be difficult to slice.

• •

162

Monster Cookies

½ cup butter
1 cup granulated sugar
1 cup plus 2 tablespoons (packed) brown
    sugar
3 eggs
2 cups peanut butter
¼ teaspoon vanilla

¾ teaspoon light corn syrup
4½ cups regular oatmeal, uncooked
2 teaspoons baking soda
¼ teaspoon salt
1 cup or 6-ounce bag chocolate chips
1 cup M & M's chocolate candies

Preheat oven to 350 degrees.

Beat butter in a mixing bowl with an electric mixer until creamy. Gradually add granulated sugar and brown sugar to butter and beat until blended. Add eggs, peanut butter, corn syrup, and vanilla and beat until blended. Add oatmeal, soda, and salt and mix until well blended. Stir in chocolate chips and M & M's.

Use an ice cream scoop to place mounds of dough 4-inches apart on a lightly greased cookie sheet. If cooking 2 sheets at a time, change racks for even browning. Bake for 12 to 15 minutes or until lightly browned.

MAKES APPROXIMATELY 48 COOKIES

• •

Secret: You can make these cookies in a variety of sizes.
The ice cream scoop makes them monster-size. If you want them smaller,
adjust the amount of dough placed on the cookie sheet before baking.

• •

Christmas Chocolate Sauce

No holiday is complete without this sauce. It is great over peppermint stick ice cream as well as straight from the jar. (It has been known to never make it to the ice cream.)

1 pound (16-ounces) bitter chocolate
    squares
6 cups sugar

1 quart cream
1 cup (2 sticks) butter, cut in 1-inch pieces
⅛ cup Cognac

Melt chocolate in a heavy pot over low heat. Add sugar and cream alternately, a little at a time, stirring well to blend. Increase the heat to medium, stir chocolate mixture until it comes to a boil and sugar is completely dissolved. Remove from heat and stir in butter pieces until melted. Add cognac and beat with a whisk until smooth. When cool store in airtight containers and refrigerate.

MAKES 2 QUARTS

Oatmeal Cherry Cookies

The extra cinnamon and dried cherries add a new twist to these classic cookies.

1 cup (2 sticks) butter, softened	½ teaspoon baking soda
1 cup (packed) brown sugar	½ teaspoon baking powder
½ cup granulated sugar	1½ teaspoons cinnamon
2 eggs	½ teaspoon salt
1 teaspoon vanilla	2 cups oatmeal, uncooked
1½ cups all-purpose flour	1 cup dried cherries

Preheat oven to 350 degrees.

Beat together butter, granulated sugar, and brown sugar in a large bowl using an electric mixer. Beat until smooth and creamy. Add eggs and vanilla continuing to beat together well.

In a medium bowl, combine flour, baking soda, baking powder, cinnamon, and salt. Add flour mixture to butter mixture beating until well mixed. Stir in oatmeal and cherries.

Drop by rounded tablespoonfuls onto ungreased cookie sheets. Bake 10 to 12 minutes or until golden brown. Remove from oven and cool 1 minute on cookie sheet. Remove from cookie sheet and finish cooling on a wire rack.

MAKES APPROXIMATELY 3 DOZEN

• •

Secret: These cookies make great ice cream sandwiches using cinnamon or vanilla ice cream. See index for Ice Cream Sandwich recipe.

• •

Tying It All Together Menu Planning

We offer our best advice about assembling a menu which suits the occasion and preserves the sanity of the hostess.

Sponsored by
Patricia and John Slaughter
in thanksgiving for
Christopher and Anne

Four Basic Parties

Getting a clue…It's like choosing a shoe!

With four basic parties any hostess can be successful:

- Coffee and Tea

- Brunch

- Dinner Party

- Cocktail Hour Party

Everything becomes an up or down computation to adjust for size, style and differing events.

Menu Planning

Menu planning is like a jig-saw puzzle; there are lots of pieces to consider:

- Tone - casual or fancy?

- Sit-down, or buffet with plates on your lap?

- How many guests to invite?

- How much time and oven space do I have?

- What do I want to make? Research, using cookbooks and cooking magazines for ideas. Think of friends' favorite foods, as well.

- Is there a theme? Italian? French? Island?

A theme often helps focus the menu, giving it continuity.

We hope readers will personalize the menus in this book to fit their own needs. For example, the tenderloin used for the cocktail party can be used at a sit down dinner. Just add a great salad and side dish. Take the recipes from the Southern Silver Coffee and use them for dessert anytime. Don't hesitate to interchange any items in these menus to suit your taste, but do substitute a vegetable for a vegetable and a starch for a starch, to maintain balance. Keep variety of color and texture in mind. Try to visualize what the plate will look like when served. Make sure to provide contrasts of sweet and savory as well.

Coffee and Tea

A dining room table draped with a beautiful linen cloth, and set with glimmering silver tea and coffee service is the epitome of elegance. It can be a great way to honor an individual or some special occasion. Actually, a Coffee and a Tea are interchangeable, albeit at different times of the day. The typical fare is small pick-up savories and delicious bite-size sweets. The larger the gathering, the more plentiful and varied the food; however, both coffee and tea are offered at both times. It is a nice idea to add punch for a large guest list, since at least a few people will want a cool drink. Weather also has a lot to do with guests' drink selections. At the very least, iced tea should be offered on a warm day.

Since our first years as a committee were spent perfecting the art of the Coffee, we have also perfected the art of small bites, portion estimates, and a thorough knowledge of what works and what does not. Actually, our mistakes have been our best teachers, and the source of laughter long after the event is past.

The art of stand-up entertaining translates to many types of parties, and we invite you to be creative within your own style parameters.

Brunch

A brunch starts the day in a relaxed festive way. The time is as flexible as the tone of the event. Feel free to pick the hour that best suits you, your guests and the type of party. It can be elegant, using fine linens, china and crystal or casual, serving on colorful paper plates in a backyard setting.

A brunch suggests a hearty meal because it is intended to take the place of breakfast and lunch. It is a great way to honor a bride and groom the day after their wedding or to entertain family and close friends following a christening. A brunch could even honor a graduate or out-of-town guests.

The day-time event is particularly conducive for multi-generational guests. Elderly persons and the very young are more at ease during the day. Many elderly people don't drive at night. Children become tired and fussy at the end of the day.

One of the nicest aspects of such an event is that so much of the food can be prepared in advance. Meat can be pre-cooked and reheated, or combination casseroles can be pre-assembled for baking. Fresh fruit can be pre-cut and refrigerated, leaving little to do at the last minute. Another positive for the budget-conscious host is the relatively low cost of brunch food and drinks. There is less likely to be an expectation of alcoholic beverages, and a pre-mixed drink or punch can easily fill the bill for those who expect one. Guests tend to drink less during the day, so even a full bar will cost less by comparison.

Dinner Party

A seated dinner party can be as casual or formal as you wish, depending upon the occasion. It's a perfect way to celebrate "round-number" birthdays, anniversaries, and holidays. Cookouts are fun, and casual outdoor dinner parties are a great way to entertain neighbors or a group of friends in warm weather.

The menu can be as elaborate or simple as the occasion demands. For a BIG birthday it is fun to go all out – starting with fabulous hors d'oeuvres, a soup or salad course, followed by the main course. Of course, you should wrap up the dinner with a spectacular dessert.

The number of people you invite depends upon your table seating arrangements. We recommend 6 to 12. If you want to entertain more people than your table accommodates, consider serving buffet style and have each guest hold his plate on his lap, which avoids having to set multiple tables, but you may do that as well, mixing the group with pre-placed name cards, and putting host and hostess at different tables or locations.

Dinner parties demand attention to the table. Centerpieces are a must, although they need not be elaborate. Conch shells and votive candles can be as effective as an elaborate floral arrangement, but flowers are a wonderful splurge for special celebrations. Even if you are not adept at floral arranging, like-colored blooms or multiple colors of the same flower can be stuffed in small containers (even cute jars!) for a lovely effect. Just make sure your guests can see each other clearly over the centerpiece.

Cocktail Hour Party

People are sometimes confused when they receive an invitation to "cocktails", a "cocktail-buffet", or a "cocktail reception". The main difference between a cocktail party and a cocktail-buffet is that there is a great deal of food served at the latter. A cocktail reception is the most formal of the three.

A cocktail party is a stand-up affair with people circulating through the rooms. It's a great way to entertain a large group of people. The party is held in the evening and usually lasts two hours. Cocktails, wine and soft drinks are served, as well as hot and cold hors d'oeuvres.

A cocktail-buffet is appropriate for a more formal occasion. It's the same as the cocktail party, but there is a buffet table with more substantial food which can serve as dinner. There should be places for guests to sit down and eat after they serve themselves at the buffet. They can eat on their laps, or small tables and chairs may be set up. A cocktail-buffet usually lasts two to three hours. The type of food served typically requires eating utensils and dinner napkins. The hosts should try to plan fork-only food for the ease of guests.

The most formal party is the cocktail reception. This type of party is most commonly used for a wedding celebration or to commemorate a special occasion. It is also appropriate for a special event, such as a party before or after a museum opening or a performing arts event. We recommend food stations along with an open bar for this type of party. The time and length of this party is determined by the event it precedes or follows, but rarely extends beyond two hours.

Such parties are service-intensive, so be prepared to have sufficient help. Bartenders, food service, kitchen prep and clean-up are all essential work assignments. When hiring people to provide such services, be sure to specify duties clearly, as well as the attire of workers. Some bartenders are willing to supply all alcohol, mixers, ice and even glassware. Be aware that you will pay for all bottles which are opened, even if only a small amount is served. Verify that remaining alcohol and mixers will be left with the host. You should be prepared to specify brands of alcohol, or whether you wish something in a particular range. Be sure to know if a guest of honor drinks a particular cocktail or brand. Don't wait until the last minute to book help. Popular, knowledgeable help are booked well in advance. Unless your home is large enough to handle a large crowd, it may be a good idea to use a private club or hotel for your party.

Southern Silver Coffee for 50

Pink Peach Champagne Punch

Black Bread with Goat Cheese and Sun-Dried Tomatoes

Smoked Turkey Breast on Tiny Orange Muffins

Pork Tenderloin Medallions with Apple Relish

Mini Bacon, Lettuce, and Tomato Tea Sandwiches

Chicken Salad Tea Sandwiches with Smoked Almonds

Steamed Fresh Asparagus with Mill's Mayonnaise

Tiny Glazed Fruit Tarts

Coconut and Toasted Almond Rum Squares

Chocolate Mousse Meringue Kisses

Cocos

Pecan Phyllo Crisps

Hot-Sweet Almonds

Candied Citrus Peel

Southern Silver Coffee

This menu is reminiscent of our traditional Silver Coffee Party. We were fortunate to have several committee members who inherited beautiful silver serving pieces and other objects d'art from their families. We love to serve and decorate with these family heirlooms. Our goal has been to prepare unique, colorful, and tasty delectables, and to keep them and the table looking as pretty as possible. Each tray can be garnished with pre-made flower or vegetable decorations, and should have at least one back-up in the kitchen for quick replacement. Since most of the food on this menu can be prepared a week ahead or the day before the Coffee, only a few finishing touches remain before serving.

We recommend serving the tea and coffee on the dining room table, covered with a beautiful linen cut-work cloth. It is best to serve everything in bite-sized pieces to prevent the necessity of a fork. It's a good idea to serve the hot and cold savories in one area and provide a separate table for desserts. It is also nice to pass some items on trays.

We like to keep our flower arrangements simple yet unique. One year the flower person used a Queen Anne chair covered with moss as the centerpiece, with the chair seat made of flowers. We always consider the style of the house and the theme of the party. We like to use unusual, show-stopping flowers in our arrangements, and have found that one or two large pieces are enough to be effective. If there is a fireplace mantle in the house, it is fun to decorate it. One year we made a miniature garden on the mantle. Another year we collected silver sugar containers and filled them with small nosegays.

A special feature of our coffee was the lagniappe, "something extra" that guests took home. We did everything from silver coffee scoops, to painted sea shells, to tiny jars of homemade marmalade. Do not limit your imagination. The hot-sweet almonds and candied citrus can be made in bulk for the lagniappe, or for Christmas or hostess gifts.

Harvest Celebration Brunch for 16

Red Roosters

Artichokes and Roasted Peppers in Toast Cups

Cruditiés - Vegetables for Dipping

Anchovy Mayonnaise

Honey Curry Dipping Sauce

Butternut Squash and Apple Soup

Autumn Turkey Salad

Grape Tomato Salad

Pumpkin Muffins with Crystalized Ginger

Maple Mousse in Chocolate Cups

Cranberry-Nut Rugalach

Harvest Celebration Brunch

What better way to say good-bye to Summer and to welcome Fall than a harvest brunch. Whether you choose a casual Saturday morning or a more formal Sunday setting, a brunch is a less ordinary and easy way to entertain. Your brunch could honor a bride or welcome new neighbors. It could also be a gathering prior to a soccer or football game.

In Florida, we have to work a little harder to provide that seasonal feeling. Table decorations are a great way to set the tone. Mound large baskets with little pumpkins, gourds, squash, and other fall vegetables. Fill in with a green trailing plant and add colorful fall leaves. This is an easy-on-the-budget centerpiece. Or you could fashion a tree from a sturdy limb, with harvest themed ornaments or fall leaves.

The Red Roosters kick off the menu with a cock-a-doodle-doo! They can be made ahead, along with the crudités and dips. Just remember to take the Red Roosters out of the freezer to defrost. The muffins and rugalach can be made ahead and frozen. The toast cups can be prepared a couple of days before the brunch. Prepare the filling for the toast cups the day before, along with the turkey salad and maple mousse. Make the soup a day ahead to reheat before serving. The morning of the brunch fill the chocolate cups and prepare the tomatoes.

This menu is best served buffet style. The night before set out the plates, silverware, napkins, glassware, pitchers, and serving pieces so you will be ready to go in the morning. Serve the soup in a tureen at the beginning of the buffet line, followed by plates for the rest of the items. Guests can hold their plate on their lap, or you can set up tables to accommodate them.

Sponsored
by
**Lisa and George
Etheridge**

New Orleans Brunch for 24

Bloody-Good Maria

Shrimp Rémoulade

Chicken Gumbo Ya Ya

Crayfish Étouffée

Shrimp-Sausage Jambalaya with Rice

Green Salad with Creole Green Onion Dressing

Bananas Foster Bread Pudding

Pralines

New Orleans Brunch

Welcome your guests with a delicious Bloody-Good Maria and a great New Orleans jazz CD playing in the background. Continue the jazz theme, or move into Mardi Gras with purple and gold feathers and masks tucked into gold-painted pots of ivy on the dining table. You might consider placing a flowering gardenia bush in a pretty cachepot on the serving table, evocative of the New Orleans Garden District, and smaller bushes on tables for a more southern-sophisticated concept. Camellias are wonderful, too, if you can find them in season.

This menu lends itself to food station serving, where guests stroll among the serving tables, helping themselves to cups of gumbo and small plates of food. Most of the dishes can be made ahead, or the ingredients put together for last minute assembly. The rémoulade, gumbo, jambalaya, and étouffée are better made the day before to let the flavors meld. Boil the shrimp the day before or order them from the fish market to save time. Be sure to cool them only slightly, then refrigerate. The salad ingredients can be put in separate plastic zip-top bags or containers to be tossed at the last minute. Make the salad dressing, bread pudding, and pralines the day before, so your last minute duties are minimal. Mix up the Bloody Marys and make the Bananas Foster sauce early the morning of the brunch. All that remains to be done is assembly.

You can be as "get-down" or "up-town" as you like with this meal, even finishing with the flourish of fine coffee and liqueurs. When we gave this party, we also offered little bags of chicory-laden coffee as a lagniappe to our parting guests. Just let the good times roll!

Sponsored
by

**Robin C.
Kuebel**

In dedication to all the great Louisiana cooks in my
family who lovingly passed on family traditions through cooking.

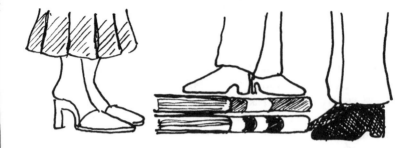

Book Club Luncheon for 12

Blush Bellini

Yummy Cheese Stars

Crab Cakes with Caper Mayonnaise and Mango Salsa

Boston Lettuce, Hearts of Palm, and Walnut Salad

Lemon Buttermilk Tart

Book Club Luncheon

Ladies have enjoyed luncheons since Queen Victoria's day! Whether the excuse is book club, bridge, or (heaven forbid) another birthday, a special lunch served in the home is so preferable to eating at a club or restaurant. A ladies' luncheon is an opportunity to use china and decorations considered too feminine for a dinner party. Floral china, dainty embroidered napkins, luncheon-sized silver, small individual flower-filled vases at each place setting, anything pink!

One Silver Sister inherited a 1950's collection of lady's head vases from her mother. They make wonderful centerpieces filled with small nosegays, and are perfect for an all girl gathering. Place three to five, depending on the size of your table, down the center. You can find reproductions that are much less expensive than the real deal, and they definitely add a bit of whimsy to any occasion.

Although the Silver Coffee committee's bridge group stopped serving drinks after we forgot one husband at the oral surgeon's office for three hours, we think it's fun to offer a special drink. For this menu we recommend Blush Bellinis to begin the festivities. This drink can be made days ahead and kept in the freezer until just before serving. The cheese stars can also be made ahead and frozen. The ingredients for the crab cakes can be assembled early in the morning, in preparation for cooking just before serving. Make the Caper Mayonnaise and Mango Salsa a couple of days ahead. The salad ingredients can be assembled a day ahead and tossed together when ready to serve. The tart can also be made the day before. Be sure to cover it well and store in the refrigerator.

A variation to the crab cake and salad menu is to top mixed greens already tossed with an oil and vinegar dressing with the crab cakes. Everything on this menu can be made ahead, allowing you time with your guests, so enjoy!

Sponsored
by
Fisher
Architects

Sip and See for 25

Kir

Five-Spice Chicken Salad in Wonton Cups

Tomato Tartlets

Cucumber Tea Sandwiches

Little Phyllo Cheesecakes

Toffee Brownies

Lemon Bars

Sip and See

The tradition of Sip and See began when a group of friends wanted to recognize and honor a mother and her second or third baby. The concept has taken off, and now most mothers and newborn children are honored in this way. This party is usually held in the late afternoon in order to accommodate working women. It is a drop-in kind of party and does not include presents. Because a group of friends is giving the party, the labor is divided. The group decides on the host home, the menu, and the cooking assignments.

This menu begins with a kir, which is a girlie libation because of its pretty pink color. The chicken salad can be made a day ahead of the party, along with the wonton cups, and assembled shortly before serving. The tomato sauce for the tomato tartlets can be made two days ahead. The tartlets can be made the morning of the party and reheated when ready to serve. They are good at room temperature as well. The cucumber sandwiches can also be prepared in the morning. Make sure you cover them with damp paper towels, wrap them well with plastic wrap, and store them in the refrigerator until ready to serve. The toffee brownies are the easiest dessert to make, and are fabulous. The lemon bars are a little more involved, but can be made ahead and frozen. The ingredients for the phyllo cheesecakes can be assembled a day or two ahead and finally assembled about four hours before the party.

Table decorations can follow the pink or blue theme, or if the new mother has her favorite colors, use them. Use children's silver cups for small nosegays and attach rattles or spoons with pink or blue ribbons.

*Sponsored
by*
**Marie and Paul
Kudelko II**

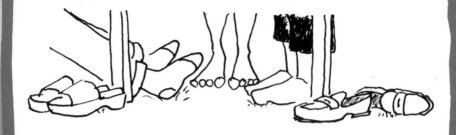

Best Friends Game Night Dinner for 10

Frozen Strawberry Daiquiri

Good-for-You Rosemary Nuts

Spinach and Artichoke Pinwheels

Open-Faced Cucumber Sandwiches

Grilled Flank Steak

Oven-Roasted New Potatoes

Spinach Gratin

Summer Salad

Almond Tart with Vanilla Ice Cream and Fresh Berries

Best Friends Game Night

Whether you invite friends for bridge, bunco, Shanghai rummy or charades, plan to serve the meal before the games begin. Featuring a special cocktail that coincides with your theme or color scheme is especially creative: Strawberry daiquiris for red, peach daiquiris for orange, blueberry for blue, etc. Daiquiris can be made ahead and frozen. The nuts, pinwheels, and tart can be made days ahead and frozen. The spinach can be prepared earlier in the week and frozen. Remember to defrost everything before baking. The berries for the tart can be made a day ahead and refrigerated. Marinate the steak early the day of the party. Prepare the salad dressing and salad ingredients in the morning and place each ingredient in separate plastic bags or covered bowls and refrigerate. When ready to serve, toss together with dressing. The potatoes can be prepared a couple of hours before guests arrive. The bread for the cucumber sandwiches can be sliced and put in plastic bags ready for last minute assembly (so they don't get soggy). The easiest way to assemble is to use a baking sheet. Place the bread squares on the sheet and spread them with mayonnaise; top with a cucumber slice and sprinkle with salt and dill. This is somewhat messy and is best contained on the baking sheet. Cover prepared sandwiches with a damp paper towel and refrigerate until ready to serve. Even the flank steak can be grilled earlier in the day, then thrown on the grill for two minutes per side to warm. Serve the steak at room temperature in warm weather and save even more time.

Even if you don't play games, this is a fabulous make-ahead menu for just plain getting together. It could even be a great potluck, with everyone making a recipe. The real point is being together and enjoying each others' company.

Sponsored
by
Silver Coffee WOW's
and
Former Committee
Members

Clearwater Fish Fry
Dinner for 12

Clearwater Harboritas

Conch Fritters with Bahamian Sauce

Ceviche with Tortilla Chips

Fried Grouper with Tropical Tartar Sauce

Garlic Cheese Grits

Maw-Maw's Slaw

Freeze-Ahead Key Lime Pie

Coconut Cream Miniature Tarts

Clearwater Fish Fry

Living in Florida provides the perfect impetus to entertain using the local catch and other fresh seafood, as well as the wonderful fresh fruits and vegetables. This menu opens the door to invite friends to your dock, backyard, or beach cottage for fresh-caught fried fish. If you don't have a fisherman in the family, get yourself on first name terms with your local fish market salesman.

This is a menu that allows everything to be done in advance so you too can enjoy the cocktails and watch the sunset while the fish is frying. The Harboritas can be made days ahead and stored in large plastic jugs in the freezer. The ceviche must be made the night before to allow it to marinate overnight. The Bahamian and tartar sauces can be made several days ahead. The grits and slaw can be prepared in the morning. Marinate the grouper in the morning as well, and prepare it for frying at the last minute. The Key Lime Pie can be made earlier in the week and frozen, and the Coconut Cream Filling can be made the day before and refrigerated for last minute assembly.

Guests will love their first taste of seafood with the Ceviche and Conch Fritters, and the excitement will continue all the way through the Key Lime Pie and Coconut Cream Tarts. This menu, of course, is adaptable to wherever you live, as the aroma of fried fish and the company of fun friends is the perfect combination for casual entertaining. During the years when we did our daytime party, we always had one item that was fried, but this has been our favorite. A couple of husbands would take turns frying, and were nick-named the "fry boys"! Don't be surprised if people nibble straight from the platter as the fish are being fried – It's just that tempting!

Keep the table setting casual and easy. Cut some palmetto leaves, use shells from the beach, put votive candles in miniature clay pots, and fill a jar with wildflowers, daisies or sunflowers. You can even cover your table with newsprint and use enamel plates and old kerosene lanterns. This kind of gathering makes it's own magic. Life is good!

Sponsored
by

**Crown
& Company,
CPA's, P.A.**

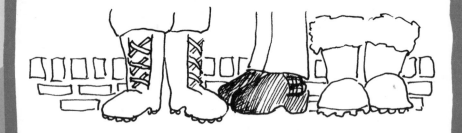

Cool Weather Warm Hearth Supper for 8

Cranberry Daiquiri

Steamed Fresh Asparagus with Tomato-Basil Dip

Mushroom, Walnut, and Gruyère Strudel Rolls

Bacon Wrapped Pork Tenderloin

Nutty Browned Brown Rice

Spinach Salad with Pine Nuts, Apples and Bacon

Rich Moist Cornbread

Old-Fashioned Apple Crisp

Cool Weather Warm Hearth Supper

When our weather turns cool enough for a fire in the fireplace, we're ready to celebrate! This supper is just perfect for such an occasion, and takes full advantage of seasonal ingredients. To establish the mood, think cozy – anything that makes you feel warm and toasty – like favorite quilts, bowls of walnuts, candles in hurricanes and brass candlesticks. You want to impart a glow, so think in reds, greens, golds, and russet tones. Cover the table with a favorite quilt or plaid blanket – or even a square of tartan wool fabric over a solid cloth. A sheath of wheat twisted and tied to resemble an hourglass makes a striking centerpiece; or carve out a pumpkin or large squash to fill with flowers. Another centerpiece idea is to fill a basket with pinecones and tuck in some pine greens. Make place cards by writing guests' names with indelible markers on real leaves. Affix them to one beautiful red apple. Tie coordinating napkins (use pinking shears to make quick ones – remember 22-inch squares are optimal) with complimentary ribbon or raffia.

This is a total make-ahead menu from the daiquiris to the apple crisp. If you like, the phyllo hors d'oeuvres, brown rice, corn bread, and apple crisp can all be prepared weeks ahead and frozen, defrosted the day before and warmed the day of the party. Prepare the daiquiris, asparagus and dip, and assemble the salad ingredients and pork tenderloin for grilling the day before. The day of the party is a breeze; you can take your time setting the table and doing final preparations and, voila! You're set to serve a fabulous warm hearth feast.

*Sponsored
by*

**The
Hart Family
Foundation**

Pacific Rim Dinner for 12

Pearl Diver Martini

Asian Beer

Scallop Dumplings

Sticky Red Curry Wings

Purchased Sushi (optional)

Sticky Ginger Beef with Rice

"California Roll" Salad

Asian Spinach Salad

Mango-Pineapple Tart with Macadamia Nut Crust

Pacific Rim Dinner

If you live in Florida, the beginnings for this party are right in your (or your neighbor's) backyard. Cut some large tropical leaves, like palm, sea grape, banana, and elephant ear. Put some of the big leaves on your table, place-mat style; the rest in tall vases. This simple all-green look works well, or if you want to add color, order some orchid sprays, ginger or bird of paradise from the florist – also a source of tropical leaves if you live in a non-tropical area. Dig out all your wood serving pieces or anything Asian inspired. Tropical fruits mounded on a wood platter make a simple centerpiece. Whichever look you go for, use low light and lots of candles for atmosphere. Close your eyes and hear the surf on Maui!

Local import shops can be a treasure trove of ideas, if you want to go a few steps more. Paper lanterns, bamboo items, and even chopsticks offer great dimension – your creativity can run as far as your wallet will let it!

The Pearl Diver Martini was a huge hit at one of our nighttime parties. Everyone wanted the recipe – so it's in the book. Serve Asian beer for the non martini drinkers. Everything on this menu can be made ahead to reheat and assemble just before the party. You can even freeze the dumplings up to two weeks. The crust, filling, and fruit for the tart can be prepared the day before, with final assembly three hours before the party.

For this party your greatest find is an Asian market – they have all the ingredients for these recipes in one place, which makes for one-stop shopping! Make a timetable for the shopping and cooking chores and do a little each day. Putting in the effort days before the party will allow you to enjoy your guests, and they will surely be impressed.

Provençal Backyard Picnic for 8

Rosé Apéritif

Coquille St. Jacques in Phyllo Cups

Marinated Olives

Roasted Eggplant Dip with Pita Crisps

Lamb Loins with Mustard Crumbs

Provençal Tomatoes

Potato-Fennel Gratin

Marinated Asparagus and Hearts of Palm Salad

Raisin Bread Pudding with Vanilla Sauce

Provençal Backyard Picnic

Transport your backyard to the south of France. Use a table large enough to seat 8 guests and cover it with traditional Provençal table linens or find country French fabric in the wonderful colors of blue, red, and, yellow to make your own. It is fun to mix these small prints using one color for an overcloth on the table, and making napkins from the other colors. Sunflowers and lavender are the flowers of Provence, and can be purchased at most grocery stores. Sunflowers make an impressive bouquet in a ceramic container or a French wire basket. If you have pottery roosters, add them to the table for a feeling of being in southern France. Use hurricane lanterns over candles or find deep votives to protect them from the wind.

Even though this is a casual, relaxed party, there is nothing casual about the food. This menu is fabulous and a lot can be made ahead. The olives can be made a month ahead. The eggplant dip and pita crisps, as well as the Coquilles St. Jacques, can be made the day before the party. Make the phyllo cups two days ahead, or make it easy on yourself and purchase them. The asparagus are best made the day before to allow them to marinate. Prepare the lamb, tomatoes and potatoes the morning of the party, refrigerate until an hour before baking, then bring them to room temperature and bake. These three dishes can sit for several minutes before serving. With this size dinner party, serve the asparagus and hearts of palm first as a separate salad course, then plate the main course and serve your guests. This menu makes a very pretty plate. The bread pudding dessert is decadent; make it early in the day, along with the vanilla sauce and refrigerate, removing them from the refrigerator when you serve the salad course. Reheat both the sauce and bread pudding slightly, as it tastes better when it's warm. Bon appetit!

Sponsored
by

**Carolyn and
Dennis Reichle**

Holiday Cocktail Buffet for 75

Open Bar

Hot Cheese Bites

Scallop Puffs

Steamed New Potatoes with Chive Butter

Pickled Shrimp

Beef Tenderloin with Mustard Horseradish Sauce

Potato-Turnip Purée

Green Beans with Caramelized Onions and Blue Cheese

Roasted Grape Tomatoes with Basil

Peppermint Ice Cream Pie

Holiday Cocktail Buffet

This menu is fabulous for Christmas, but equally wonderful for any special occasion. It would work well for a couples' bridal shower or a round-numbered birthday, and is designed for entertaining in your home. If you are not comfortable doing all the food yourself, hire a caterer and give them your recipes or make some items yourself and parcel out the rest. This gives your party a more personal and, therefore, very special touch.

Holidays are a special time to get together with family and friends to celebrate what is meaningful. It is also a great time to entertain because our houses are all decorated for Christmas.

The focal point of this party is the dining room table. To make it beautiful gather all your crystal pieces: vases (small and large), decanters, candlesticks, and votives. Special order Christmas holly with red berries and stems of amaryllis. Fill crystal containers with water and put holly and amaryllis in them. Place five containers down the center of the table. Arrange candlesticks and votives, with white or ivory candles, among the flower-filled containers. This is very easy to do and makes an impressive table without breaking the budget.

Both the cheese bites and pie can be made ahead and frozen. The shrimp needs to be made several days ahead. The scallop puff ingredients and potato-turnip purée, can be made one day ahead and refrigerated. Store the toast rounds in airtight containers. The potato filling can be prepared several days in advance. Cook the potatoes, fill, and garnish them the day before the party; cover them well and refrigerate. The tomatoes can be prepared for baking early in the morning. The green beans are best served at room temperature and can also be made early in the day and assembled just before serving. The scallop puffs should be assembled and broiled just before serving. The beef can be roasted before the guests arrive and served at room temperature. We recommend having at least one or two helpers in the kitchen to help assemble and pass hors d'ouevres, as well as assembling and placing the main dishes on the dining table. For more information on this type of entertaining, turn to the Easy Steps to Entertaining section.

Special Occasion Reception for 150

Red and White Wine

Open Bar

Marinated Vodka Drinks

• • • First Course • • •

Snow Pea Soup

• • • Salmon Station • • •

Smoked Salmon with Capers, Chopped Red Onion,
and Dill-Mustard Sauce

Citrus Marinated Hearts of Palm Salad

• • • Sandwich Station • • •

Mini Fried Grouper Sandwiches on
Tiny Parker House Rolls with Caper Mayonnaise

Shaved Ham on Tiny Rye Rolls with Hot Mustard

Breast of Turkey or Tenderloin on
Tiny Soft Egg Bread Knots with Hot Mustard

• • • Lamb Chop Station • • •

Grilled Baby Lamb Chops

Beet and Orange Salad with Citrus Vinaigrette

• • • Pasta Station • • •

Seafood Lasagna

Lasagna with Tomato-Cream Sauce and Mozzarella

Romaine Lettuce with Prosciutto Crisps

• • • Dessert Station • • •

Banana Strudel

Pineapple Upside-Down Cake

Chocolate Truffle Tart with Pecan Caramel Sauce

• • • Specialty Coffee Station • • •

*Sponsored
by*
**Silver Coffee WOW's
and
Former Committee
Members**

Special Occasion Reception

There are many special occasions to celebrate in life. Engagements, weddings, wedding anniversaries, and round-numbered birthdays are among the important ones. This menu is reminiscent of those we create for our evening event. You may use it as is or use parts of it to create a memorable party. This party is suitable for entertaining at home or at a club. You can prepare and assemble the food yourself, hire a caterer, or if using a club have the club's chef prepare your menu.

When guests first arrive, pass trays of glasses of red and white wine. This frees up the bartenders and expedites everyone getting a drink. We have suggested marinated vodka drinks, which can be served at their own station. The first time we served them at one of our parties they were a big hit. Guests help themselves. For 150 people you would set up two to three bars, plus the vodka station.

The first item on this menu is snow pea soup, which is served warm in small glasses or cups, and passed on trays to guests. There is no need for a spoon, as the soup is simply sipped.

When planning a large party, we like to have our food set up in individual stations. Each station features a mini-meal. The stations are equipped with small plates, forks, and napkins. While this is essentially a stand-up party, it is nice to have several tables and chairs for people who wish to sit while they eat. When you plan a large reception, your best friend is the rental company, where it is easy to rent everything you need. We have even rented a coffee vendor's cart (and his services) for our nighttime party. This has always been a huge hit.

The salmon station and sandwich station involve assembling food. Use the fried grouper recipe for the grouper sandwiches. The shaved ham and turkey can be purchased, as well as the various rolls. Plan to serve 75 of each. Many of the other station items can be prepared ahead. Consult the recipes and plan accordingly - figure out how many times a recipe has to be made to accommodate the crowd. We have made some recommendations following the recipes for this party.

It is important to have enough help. The rule of thumb is one helper per 50 to 60 guests. It is also helpful to have several large plastic-lined baskets on hand for guests' dirty dishes. For more details about entertaining a large crowd, go to the Easy Steps to Entertaining section.

Flowers and decorations can be as simple or elaborate as you wish. Weddings usually demand going all out or as much as your budget permits. Consulting with an excellent florist can relieve anxiety about decor. For our parties, we like to have at least two show-stopping arrangements, and the rest of the decor can be more subtle. We like to use lots of votive candles which provide great ambience and are easy on the budget.

Index

Index

Index

S

No Small Feat!

• •

Children's Home Society of Florida
Gulf Coast Division
8306 Laurel Fair Circle, Suite 160
Tampa, Florida 33610
Phone: 813.740.4266
www.chsfl.org

Name

Street Address

City   State   Zip

Phone

Your Order	Quantity	Total
No Small Feat! at $24.95 per book		$
Sales tax at $1.75 per book		$
Shipping and handling at $4.00 per book		$
Total		$

Method of Payment: ❑ VISA   ❑ MasterCard   ❑ American Express
                      ❑ Check payable to Children's Home Society of Florida
                      (Write "Cookbook" on the memo line.)

Account Number

Cardholder Name

Signature
                    Photocopies accepted.

No Small Feat!

• •

Children's Home Society of Florida
Gulf Coast Division
8306 Laurel Fair Circle, Suite 160
Tampa, Florida 33610
Phone: 813.740.4266
www.chsfl.org

Name

Street Address

City   State   Zip

Phone

Your Order	Quantity	Total
No Small Feat! at $24.95 per book		$
Sales tax at $1.75 per book		$
Shipping and handling at $4.00 per book		$
Total		$

Method of Payment: ❏ VISA   ❏ MasterCard   ❏ American Express
❏ Check payable to Children's Home Society of Florida
(Write "Cookbook" on the memo line.)

Account Number

Cardholder Name

Signature

Photocopies accepted.